Sunward I've Climbed

BOOKS BY HERMANN HAGEDORN

Verse

A TROOP OF THE GUARD AND OTHER POEMS

POEMS AND BALLADS

THE GREAT MAZE AND THE HEART OF YOUTH

LADDERS THROUGH THE BLUE

THIS DARKNESS AND THIS LIGHT
HARVARD POEMS, 1907–1937

COMBAT AT MIDNIGHT

Biography

ROOSEVELT IN THE BAD LANDS

LEONARD WOOD

THE MAGNATE
WILLIAM BOYCE THOMPSON AND HIS TIME

BROOKINGS

EDWIN ARLINGTON ROBINSON

THE BUGLE THAT WOKE AMERICA
THE SAGA OF THEODORE ROOSEVELT'S LAST BATTLE FOR HIS COUNTRY

SUNWARD I'VE CLIMBED
THE STORY OF JOHN MAGEE

Novels

FACES IN THE DAWN

BARBARA PICKS A HUSBAND

THE ROUGH RIDERS

Juveniles

YOU ARE THE HOPE OF THE WORLD!

THE BOYS' LIFE OF THEODORE ROOSEVELT

WE THE PEOPLE: THE TEN DREAMS OF ZACH PETERS

THE BOOK OF COURAGE

John Gillespie Magee, Jr.

Sunward I've Climbed

The Story of John Magee
poet and soldier
1922-1941

BY

HERMANN HAGEDORN

NEW YORK
THE MACMILLAN COMPANY
1943

Fourth Printing

PRINTED IN THE UNITED STATES OF AMERICA
BY THE VAIL-BALLOU PRESS, INC., BINGHAMTON, N. Y.

To

JOHN and FAITH MAGEE

BRAVE, SELFLESS AND CANDID,

THIS STORY OF THEIR SON IS DEDICATED

IN ADMIRATION AND FRIENDSHIP

FOREWORD

It has been possible to tell the story of this youth, so exceptional in his gifts, so typical of thousands of his contemporaries in his conflicting aims and inner turmoil, only because his father and mother, the Reverend John Gillespie Magee and Mrs. Magee, of Washington, D.C., were not only willing to have the story honestly told, but, from their memories of their son and the letters he wrote from Rugby, themselves provided the illuminating details. Except as otherwise indicated, the letters in the fourth section, "The Flier," are all addressed to them.

Mr. Hugh Lyon, headmaster of Rugby School in England, has, in his discriminating account of young John's years at the great English school, provided not only colorful detail but the basic outlines of the picture; and Mr. J. V. Hitchcock, headmaster of St. Clare School, Walmer, Kent, has told movingly of John's earlier schooling. Mr. Geoffrey Sergeant, of Trinity College, Cambridge, now of South Africa, has written, as only he could, of the high peak of John's boyhood.

Other friends, notably Mr. Lawrence Viles, of New York, Mr. Robert Dawson, of North Carolina, Mr. Warner Gookin, of Oak Bluffs, Massachusetts, Mr. Francis H. Bangs, of Litchfield, Connecticut, Mrs. Wilson Plumer Mills, Mrs. W. P. Roberts, and the Reverend and Mrs. J. C. Thomson, of Nanking and New York, the Reverend R. Brooke Stabler, Mr. Paul Child, Mrs. Marion Meigs Hyde, Mr. Max Stein, and Dean Sears of the Avon School, Avon, Connecticut, have contributed illuminating reminiscences or helped the author in other ways. To them all, and not least to Miss Ruth Lachman, who typed the successive drafts of the book, he offers his thanks.

H. H.

CONTENTS

THE MIRACLE

At thirty thousand feet, the mounting exhilaration of his spirit blew off in singing words:

*"Oh! I have slipped the surly bonds of Earth
And danced the skies on laughter-silvered wings. . . ."*

Like a great hawk he wheeled and dipped and soared, swung in vast arcs, drew majestic circumferences around his personal empyrean. His heart was singing, and his mind, too. A sonnet was being born. First, the octave that should paint the picture, the picture of himself, John Magee, chasing "the shouting wind along", flinging his "eager craft through footless halls of air". Then the sextet, soaring in joyous freedom,

"Up, up the long, delirious, burning blue",

straight to the crystalline summation.

The rhymes dropped into place. No groping of the pinched imagination for sounds that matched and made a pattern. The jubilant mind, soaring high, reached deep into the resources of the unconscious. The flier grounded the plane and, as he strode off to his quarters, the final, fourteenth line came, firing the whole with meaning.

Not a line yet on paper, but fourteen glowing lines in his head. He wrote the poem on the back of a letter to his father and mother in America: "I thought it might interest you."

A boy's sonnet, to be published somewhere, sometime,

3

perhaps, and read by a handful who like such things. A boy's expression of exhilaration, bursting at the end into flame. A boy's votive candle on the high altar. Exultant, beautiful words, but words only. Winsome, as all youth is winsome, when it forgets itself and reaches clean, bright hands to the God it hopes but is not sure exists. But what is fragile loveliness in the midst of an epochal struggle for mastery? A bird's feather floating down in No Man's Land, a birdsong in the intervals of the cannonade.

Over the training-field the planes soar, dip and tumble. A plane roars out of a cloud. Two planes, two gallant youths, crash. . . .

Yes, he has "slipped the surly bonds of earth".

And the sonnet?

The sparkling words have suddenly become something else. They are not words at all any more. They are a life, a gallant, gifted, laughing life, offered for freedom. And they are more. They are youth everywhere, slipping the "surly bonds" of egocentric living, soaring up from a world where money, pleasure, a career, living one's own life, are important, into a broader, cleaner atmosphere of self-surrender and self-giving, and a freedom beyond any earthly freedom, with eternity no farther away than the outstretched hand.

The inspired words are all this. And they are yet more. They are hearts throughout the world, hungering, too, to slip "the surly bonds of earth", climb sunward,

"*Where never lark, or even eagle flew*",

and, amid ruin and impending ruin, put out a hand and touch the face of God.

THE POEM

HIGH FLIGHT

Oh! I have slipped the surly bonds of Earth
   And danced the skies on laughter-silvered wings;
Sunward I've climbed, and joined the tumbling mirth
   Of sun-split clouds,—and done a hundred things
You have not dreamed of—wheeled and soared and swung
   High in the sunlit silence. Hov'ring there,
I've chased the shouting wind along, and flung
   My eager craft through footless halls of air. . . .

Up, up the long, delirious, burning blue
   I've topped the wind-swept heights with easy grace,
Where never lark, or even eagle flew—
   And, while with silent, lifting mind I've trod
   The high untrespassed sanctity of space,
Put out my hand and touched the face of God.

THE BOY

By rights, he should have been a complete international-
ist, with no roots anywhere. For his mother was English and
his Scotch-Irish father was born in Pittsburgh and had for
years been a Protestant Episcopal missionary in China,
when his son was born in Shanghai. John's first playmates
were Chinese, except for a long summer when politics got
even hotter than the weather in China and a kindergarten
in Japan provided satisfactory substitutes. It was, incidentally, in that kindergarten that Ian, as his elders called him,
remembering his Scottish ancestry, discovered the other
sex. The little Japanese girl was only the first of many to
stir his susceptible heart, but she was magic while the fervor
lasted. Yet, even so, he had to be watched, lest he push her
into the deep end of the swimming-pool.

He was a personality from his earliest years, with his shining eyes, his voluble tongue and his quick intelligence
which, even at the age of four, set his father one day
feverishly searching his orthodoxy for an adequate answer
to what seemed, at first, a very simple query. The elder had
been praying at his son's bedside, praying specifically that,
whatever came, he and his little John, who was inclined to
be scary after nightfall, might not be afraid. "Daddy," commented the boy, "if we ask the Lord not to let me be afraid,
and I *am* afraid, what?" The question proved more and
more disconcerting to the elder, the farther he pursued it.

From the beginning John had a strong antipathy for the

humdrum. At Hillcrest, the American cooperative school
in Nanking, when he was eight, the cultivated and intuitive
woman who was given the task of keeping "that Magee
boy" out of mischief learned that the rangy youngster with
the rapier-like mind had to be given something to think
about that seemed to him important or he would be fighting the Chinese boys and making himself objectionable in
divers other ways.

His teachers were conscious of a "soaring mind" and,
when they challenged it, he was tractable and cooperative.
But the headlong boy had to be kept interested, reaching
always a little beyond his powers, or he was in trouble. He
learned faster than other children and invented deviltry
while they were catching up.

It was the same at St. Clare School in England's south-
eastern shire, Kent, where he was sent when he was nine.
St. Clare was a "preparatory school", not in the American
sense of a secondary school, preparing for college, but a
grammar school, preparing for those "public schools", like
Rugby, Harrow and Eton, which are the antithesis of what
Americans mean by the term, being private schools of a
peculiarly exclusive character, preparing English boys for
the university and for public life.

"He was always aiming at the stars", the headmaster of
St. Clare, J. V. Hitchcock, warm of heart and firm of hand,
wrote of John Magee after his death. "Even at the end of
his time with us, he was only just in his teens, and had not
realized that the way was difficult. At first it was the glitter that attracted him. Scholastically, he was far above the
average, but his mercurial disposition would not allow him
to concentrate on certain details."

No, Johnny Magee just naturally didn't concentrate on details. "The Head" did what he could about it, and it took all that he had of wisdom and patience. The boy was volatile, jumping at any mischief anyone else proposed and ready to suggest deviltries of his own when other imaginations flagged. He got his first beating for exploding a blank cartridge in class because he did not like the teacher, and his second for publicly mimicking the same objectionable preceptor.

He grew fast in body; even faster in mind; not so fast in spirit. But he did grow. A boyish timidity gradually gave way, under the weight of the school tradition that you took what came without squawking. "His football has improved," "the Head" wrote John's father when John was thirteen, "because he has been ready to meet opposition and not just avoid it. He is still excitable," the headmaster continued, "and ready for any new idea, but he is also far more ready to see the possible folly of it, and to admit it."

John was interested enough in the classics to shine without apparent effort, and was fluent, if "somewhat flamboyant", in composition. But he withered in routine. He learned to play the piano creditably in a single term, for he was full of music, but in the face of the music-master's laments, stubbornly resisted the tedium of learning to read notes.

The headmaster was a wise man in his day and generation and opened Kentish windows on the troubled world outside. "If you want peace," he had a way of saying, "prepare for war." "But," wrote one of John's schoolmates, years later, "what with the 'pinko' tendencies of English boys

at the time, he had a hard time convincing us young ideal-
ists of the soundness of his doctrine. We had faith in him,
though, and it was to him that John showed his earliest
efforts at poetry after he had gone to Rugby."

2

Rugby taught John Magee to write and stimulated him to think. The headmaster, Hugh Lyon, was a poet of considerable distinction, and he took the gifted, thirteen-year-old American boy under his wing. "The Head" had a number of children, of which the youngest, Jill, aged four, chose to give John her particular devotion. Of all the boys who came to visit the family, John, she contended, had "the bestest face", but her father suspected that it was John's way of holding philosophical discourses with her, while she was having her supper in bed, that won her heart.

There was another girl, a year older than John—more than a year in maturity—the daughter of a Rugby master, who was to all intents and purposes a member of the family. Her name was not Diana, but that will serve. She wrote poetry, and let him see it. There was a tender thing she called "Spring Night", which Alice Meynell would have cherished.

> "A milky phosphorescence hangs
> Above the apple-trees,
> Pale as the gleam that haunts the foam
> At night, in shallow seas.
> Shepherds made love in Arcady
> Beneath such boughs as these.
>
> "The Plough bestrides the heavenly field
> Beyond the ancient hill;
> Like nameless flowers of the night

The stars hang clear and chill;
Below them, in benighted hearts
All mortal fires are still.

"Till day revive their dreaming flame,
Let human longings sleep;
The apple-blossom gleams, the trees
Stand in enchantment deep;
And all above, a million stars
Eternal vigil keep."

There were picnics, and visits at the Lyons', in the Lake District and in Yorkshire, in vacations. Johnny learned to breathe in the rarefied atmosphere of brilliant intellectual give-and-take, retaining a charming gaiety which does not always accompany the quick intellect in the very young; and for the fair Diana conceived a more or less speechless admiration.

He did well in his studies, which meant something at Rugby where standards were high, and was frequently at or near the head of his form. His first exultant report to his parents, "In this school we can do exactly what we like," proved erroneous, and he found, behind a generous outward freedom, an exacting and uncompromising discipline. Rugby had traditions—centuries of them—and its greatest focussed about the mighty Thomas Arnold, creator of the English "public school", and patron saint, generation after generation, of American "prep schools", too, Arnold, superbly dead in his great son's immortal "Lines" and, eighty years later, indecently exhumed by the ironic pen of Lytton Strachey to make a cynics' holiday. John found Rugby something to live up to, and it took a boy who was at least half English to accept without a struggle the distinctions and taboos, bewildering to outsiders but full of meaning to those concerned, which generations of boys had hardened into established custom.

John was inclined to be restive under the control of his elders, but, having enjoyed some preliminary training at St. Clare, where the older boys mercilessly bullied the younger in the best "public school" tradition, slipped comfortably into a system in which the controls were more rigid than any an adult would dare decree, and found that he liked Rugby. Rugby, in its turn, discovered in Johnny Magee a friendly soul who had a way of looking you in the eyes and saying exactly what he meant, enjoying life to the full and throwing himself with abandon into everything that came along, without much reflection or control.

On excursions into the English countryside, the headmaster became aware of the aspiration behind the ebullience of act and speech, and to appreciate the adventurous spirit, chafing under restraint. "When he was rebellious (he often was)," the headmaster wrote subsequently, "it would be because he was not allowed to attempt a dangerous climb or too long an expedition; but he couldn't be sulky for long."

Halfway through his first term his house-master described him as "intelligent, volatile, emotional, untidy, thoughtless, keen", but gradually the unrelated qualities and impulses drew together and became a personality, infused with a spirit which could never apparently be satisfied unless it was reaching toward something away out of sight. He was still the boy of the Nanking school who knew that

*"A man's reach must exceed his grasp
Or what's a heaven for?"*—

the boy of St. Clare, reaching for the stars, entranced by the glitter, and, in the intervals of aspiration, behaving like Sam Scratch. He saw himself fairly clearly, both the lift and the downward pull. "I hope you don't think I'm being a spend-thrift", he wrote his mother, early in his Rugby career. "I do try to spend less now than I did on first coming to the School. But I have so many failings that they completely bewilder me sometimes. Still—I hope one day I will learn to control them. I have learnt a lot of varied lessons this term, and hope I will be the better for them. I sometimes have glimpses of what a help I could be here and at home, but it will need real effort to make that dream come true."

As he gradually fitted himself into the life of the great school, he grew in steadiness and industry and began to show promise in English and the classics. His form-master spoke of his "lively, intelligent work", marred by "a certain restlessness and excess of ambition." The teacher of Scripture found him "helpful and sometimes combative in discussion", his English teacher "promising", with some originality of idea. "What he has to learn is restraint, both in matter and manner, and more patience in criticism."

"He was still impatient of drudgery and detail," the headmaster recorded, "but he had a shrewd eye for what mattered in life and in work. He was still uncontrolled in opinion and occasionally did wild things; one night, for instance, he climbed out on to School House roof and tied a label with his name on it to the hand of the School clock. But, when he did kick over the traces, he was so charmingly penitent that it was easy to forgive him."

3

"I have been doing a lot of thinking," John, aged thirteen, wrote his mother. "I have discovered that, if I could only exercise enough will-power to dig it out, I have got a fairly vivid imagination. I think that, in time, I will learn to express it on paper. I often try now, but somehow just fail to 'click'. But I think that if I can once master a strong enough vocabulary, I might be able to do something with it."

His first attempts were what might be expected, wooden and consciously "poetic", but gradually, in the periodic chores of a composition course which included practice with verse, his articulation began to unlimber. He began to feel the excitement of pursuit of the elusive image, the word always a little beyond the reach.

> "I stood alone
>   And stared into a starlit sky,
>   Hearing only the hum
>   Of distant worlds, whirling
>   Silently through space; and suddenly
>   I knew! Adumbral Truth
>   Took shape before my eyes, appearing
>   Out of nothingness,
>   Glimmering through a world of dark,
>   Chimeric fancy. Its voice
>   Re-echoed down the ages, wave

Upon wave of
Swelling sound, until the stars
In their gigantic unison
Took up the strain, and all the sky
Was filled with a deep,
Pellucid chorus . . . then it ceased,
And all the thrill of revelation
Sank into the obscurity of
Reason . . .
And I gazed up into the
Cold, hard faces of the stars."

The headmaster recognized, in the gay-hearted, contradictory personality, a poet in embryo, and led him on; and the lovely Diana provided all the inspiration required. "He began writing poetry," noted the headmaster, "of a sincerity and extravagance which mirrored his nature." If the influence of Rupert Brooke was clear, there was a reason beyond the natural appeal to youth of the romantic poet-hero whose far-off grave was "forever England". For Brooke had been born at Rugby, the son of one of the masters, had played cricket and football for the school and won its poetry prize. When John Magee turned to him for inspiration, he turned, in a sense, to an elder brother.

Johnny set no dates on the poems he printed by his own hand when he was seventeen, except as he stated that all were written between the ages of thirteen and sixteen, "when Wonder was fighting for life in the teeth of pride, and Love lay shivering under the howling winds of adolescent cynicism" (thus, capitals and all). "Lines written on a Sleepless Night" were young, but older poets have done worse, and some of the great have done considerably worse, between thirteen and sixteen:

"I love the moon's soft mist-encircled light;
It weaves a silver spell; the very leaves
Seem turned to silver-stone!—surely tonight
There's something strange abroad! Beneath the eaves
Thrushes are nestling,—hushed; and these I love;
And, too, I love thin spires of smoke, that rise
Like incense to the stars; and then, to move
When all the world's asleep, or to surprise
A wakeful mouse from some close hiding place . . .
I love to think I hear an angel's voice
Hung on the whisper of the wind. This place,
This night, this hour, this sky, are all my choice!
I love the earth, the sea, the heaven above,
But, more than these, the right to say I love!"

Whether he had the right or not, he said it in varying sharps and flats, but mainly in the sonnet's stately measure.

"I will not say that men will not forget you,
Nor boast that your brown eyes will never fade;
I should be living, had I never met you,
But I'd have lived alone, and in the shade. . . .
I will not praise your laugh, your graceful walking,
Nor say that death will never close your eyes . . .
There have been those who praised a woman's talking
—Said it would live for ever. These were lies.

"The time will come, dear heart, when suddenly laughter
Dies on the lips, glad hair turns quickly grey;

And friends *will have forgotten shortly after—*
But I shall say, that once your skin was fair,
And as you stood beside me in the trees
A petal fluttered down upon your hair . . ."

Immature? Of course. But genuine. This was no manu-
factured emotion, no literary exercise. This boy was experi-
encing the delight of first love and somehow managing to
get it into words so something of the fragrance remained.

"I think if God had heard my foolish prayer,
And you had loved me as I hoped you would;
And I'd looked up one day and seen you there,
—And you had smiled, as if you understood
Those dreams that I had always feared profane,
And did not mind;—and if I had but found
The quiet touch of your hand, to keep me sane
When all the long, familiar faces frowned . . .

"Then, on some cool and secret-shadowed night
I'd wake, and find in your remembered eyes
The strange new Truth I'd longed to realize—
As when some ploughman strikes a precious stone,
And holding it intensely in his hand
With sudden sweetness knows it for his own."

He was living obviously with the elder poets, who still
had time and space for elaborate imagery, but he was reaching out toward the latter-day voices.

"I have been reading a good bit of Modern Poetry lately,"
he wrote his mother, "because up till now I have always
regarded myself as being a little prejudiced against Mod-

ern Verse. Well, I have been both pleased and disappointed; pleased, because it seems to have a kind of freshness which was not evident in the older style; it all seems vitally alive and always conscious of life; and disappointed, partly because I think it is often rather sensual, and partly because there seems to be a sad want of the old beauty of thought and expression." He had been arguing this point, he added, with his English master who was an enthusiast for the moderns. "He thinks that poetry is only an expression of life, and that, since life today is seldom beautiful, therefore poetry is tending to stick to reality and go along the same road. My point is, however, that poetry is an *escape* from life rather than an expression of it. There's so little in life that's worth expressing nowadays, so why try?"

4

Life unquestionably is very drab and unromantic—at sixteen; or the opposite; or both at the same moment. John,
it happened, was having an extraordinarily good time, with
football and tennis and riding and rifle-practice and sailing—sailing on the Channel in his own dingy in vacations,
best of all—and acting in school plays. . . . "He made a
great success of a difficult part in 'Judgment Day' ", wrote
the headmaster. "I have often thought he would have
made the perfect Hamlet". . . . . All this, inextricably min-
gled with poetry and the wonder of windows opening on
new areas of an entrancing and difficult world, and the effort to get a headful of exciting ideas somehow on a sheet
of white paper.

"I have been rather worried about life in general the
last two or three days," he wrote his father and mother. "I
can't sleep at night when I'm worried; I can never go to
sleep without settling my little problems; so the only thing
I have done has been to get up and walk around in the
small hours of the morning. Incidentally, I find that this is
the best time of day (or night!) for writing poetry. In-
spirations are not hard to find when the moon is sailing
high above the clouds at midnight. . . . I don't think
words can describe my sensations at standing by an open
window watching the moon when 'all this mighty heart is
lying still'—when the only sound abroad is the stirring of
the wind in the elms on the Close. I sometimes wonder why

men were made to sleep at night. It is a time when something strange, something indescribable, is abroad . . . something which the powers of man can't attain or even begin to understand, and I won't be satisfied until I have found out what it is.

"Enough of this nonsense. I expect you think I'm mad, or too young to control my emotions; on the other hand, perhaps you understand. I don't know."

So he poured it all into verse.

"This is a monstrous night!
It presses in my ears, my eyes,
As if to crush out
My very soul. I hear no sound
Except the urgent
Ticking of a clock, and some busy whisper
Of the wind. Above, the stars
Have hid their faces from my eyes. The aspen moon
Slips silently behind a cloud
As if afraid to shine; and somewhere in this thick,
Unfathomable gloom, there is
Reality.
Its shape, its form, its depth
I can not know; incomprehensible,
A feeling, not a thing; but this I know:
A hand stretched out to mine. I heard a Voice
Whispering a secret to my soul. . . ."

"Some day," the Head said to him, "you're going to write much better poetry than I am writing."

That was pure intuition, on the basis of inconclusive

evidence, and strong meat for a boy of sixteen. But "the Head" knew his Johnny, knew the aspiration, the ardor, knew, above all, that, behind all the brilliancy and imagination, were self-doubt and bewilderment, which required a shot in the arm.

"You know, it seems to me that there is something essentially, even elementally wrong, about school life," John was writing his father and mother at the opening of what was to prove his final year at Rugby. "Just now is the time when a boy is at his most impressionable stage, and yet, at the same time, he has to fight some of the hardest battles of his life (How I hate that expression!). Just when he is trying to form good habits, he is thrust out to face a lot of bad ones (and wherever you have a lot of boys living together you always find bad habits, whether you like to admit it or not). It seems so illogical. He goes to a school such as this, which may in itself be admirable, but simply turns a lot of sausages out of a machine, consisting of what we are pleased to call the 'public school type'! Here a boy's emotions, desires, hopes, everything, get swallowed up in the great Quest of Work—however unconstructive and abysmal; and he's darn lucky if they ever revive again. Youth gets squashed down by the whims and wills of Age, in the shape of a fat old man with a mortar board and gown.

"Now is the time when a boy sees life at its best, untainted by the sordidness of age. Then why can't he have time to enjoy the beauties of bird, beast, and flower? If I were to die tomorrow, how much of Beauty would I have seen? Pathetically little. When I shall probably never be more appreciative, more happy, more able to see a thing in its natural beauty, without having to think of its position

with regard to '*autres choses*', its significance in life, etc.
And how do I spend my time? Sitting before a pile of books
and trying to concentrate on Demosthenes to the exclu-
sion of all the thrills I might have at beholding something
beautiful, something real, something natural. School con-
sists of the worship of man and the things he has made; his
books, his letters, his thoughts. Plenty of time, we say for
Beauty afterwards. Suppose there is no 'afterwards'?"

Yes, indeed. Suppose?

5

As with many adolescents, the romantic contemplation of death occupied a mind which to his companions seemed perennially gay. As spring approached, John was working on a dramatic poem with which he was hoping to capture the Rugby poetry prize. Its opening has the haunting melancholy of the initial lines of *"Der Tor und der Tod"*, written by another boy of seventeen, Hugo von Hofmannsthal, though there is no indication that John had ever read the Austrian's elegy of youth and twilight and spring.

"What agony of Beauty! How the sad,
  Long look of moonlight touches all this place;
  A crazy sweetness fills my head, until
  The mind is swamped with fullness of the soul . . .
  How will this beauty, at the time of death
  Engulf the mind that once beheld its form!
  How will this quiet hour in after years
  Come sweeping back, come flooding over me!
  What more could man desire?
                    "—Quiet, and Peace,
  You I would have flow over me like water,
  As some cool wave upon a sun-dried sand.
  Here is a soothing rest for the troubled mind
  In evening's coolness, fingers of the wind . . .
  For here, in this freshening hour of breeze and night-birds,
  Here is the source of our constant sanity

We who spend years in offices and cars
Who, though the slaves of Time, can yet sustain
The balance of our twisted nerves and notions
As a heated lover, hearing the song of a bird,
Is still; hears too, perhaps, though undefined,
The haunting drift of death in the sombre wind . . .
How many generations loved this place,
And, passing, left to us this privilege?
So we who have come, continuing in their stead,
Inherit the spirit and phrase of ancient sagas,
Hearing, perhaps, in the whisperings of leaves
Tales that our fathers told when they were here,
Feeling, perhaps, at evening in this place
Loves of the morning that our fathers knew
Here where the valley is filled with voices and pine-
    winds . . ."

He completed the poem in the spring vacation under
the influence of a distinguished and high-minded scholar
he had recently met, possibly at Rugby. He was C. Franklin
Angus, vice-master of Trinity College—guide, philosopher
and friend to countless Cambridge students—who invited
him to join a reading-group at Mortehoe, a quiet village
perched above the rocky North Devon coastline. The four
others of the party were college undergraduates, all years
older than John, absorbed in the European crisis, moving
towards war, and asking the deepest questions of life. Among
them was a young South African named Geoffrey Sergeant,
to whom Johnny felt instantly drawn. Before breakfast, on
the morning following his arrival, he was on the summit of
Morte Point with the young Cantabrigian. They had both

been trained in the habits of what is known as "the reserve of the British", and it was astonishing to both to find themselves talking in terms of complete understanding. "Never before or since," wrote Sergeant later, "have I known such inspiration and intimacy in the sharing of ideas. It was very wonderful, the sheer spontaneity and candour of it all."

The evening also of that first day they spent together on Morte Point, talking until the long northern twilight closed in on them and the stars broke over the sea and midnight was come, thrashing through the great questions of life. What is God, what is Man? What is love, what is death? What is it to live significantly, creatively? How does Man express his highest self, to God, to humanity, to country? What if the narrower and the wider loyalties conflict? How far can inequality and privilege be justified?

"On such things," Sergeant wrote later, "did we speak—not, of course, agreeing in all details, which is why we helped each other to see so much farther than when alone: but we achieved the deepest unity of understanding that I have ever known. I felt quite emancipated from the body, and from the limits of space and time. Certainly for me, the intensity of the experience has hardly lessened, although, as I write, it was three years ago. John and I were striving after the same ideal, the Christian ideal, which illuminates and transcends mere ethics, and which seems to be the only common denominator for human reconstruction. To the problems that we discussed we brought our different contributions: I, the more intricate and reasoned fabric of the older student; John, the more vividly direct awareness, and the poet's insight and power of creative expression. Even at seventeen, John's power to inspire, to see in the dark, was altogether exceptional and perhaps unique."

In the morning-light, only a few hours after the end of their night-long exchange of ideas and aspirations, they climbed Morte Point once more. It was Good Friday. On the morning of Easter Day they attended the Communion Service together in the little church of St. Mary.

Day after day, through the vacation, reading together in the mornings, tramping over the downs in the afternoons or frisking along the great stretch of Woolacombe sands, they were aware of an ominous sense of impending war. John remarked that he expected to die young. Yet he was happy, ebulliently happy. As they stood in the crisp, damp air where the downs met the sea, speaking of life and death and the resurrection, they came upon a little lamb, which delighted John and he lifted it tenderly in his arms.

For ten days John walked on air. He had a way of taking the color of his surroundings, of tuning his mind to the pitch of the people he was with—a Magee trait which had produced numerous successful politicians—and he basked in the straight warm beams of uncompromising idealism. In this spirit he would live, in this spirit he *must* live, in this spirit he had a contribution to make.

"With other friends than John I have in youth been sharing the greatest things in life," Geoffrey wrote John's mother after John's death. "Link by link, our ideals have been forged—sailing orders for a Brave New World. Slowly and dimly the vision began to form. Writing, scaling the mountains, tramping the hilltops, in England, South Africa, and parts of Europe; thrashing out problems far into the night in our rooms in Cambridge, slowly and hardly, in an age of chaos and crisis, others and I strove for an ideal. The fragments we could see clearly enough, but the whole remained yet blurred and there was none among us great enough to express, as a whole, the separate ideas in which we believed.

"Then I met John, and he it was, with his vivid insight, his beautiful, creative vision, who, for me, did more than any other to bring the whole picture into focus. He became and remains the most lovable and the most inspiring of my friends, the companion with whom above all I wished to face the difficult tasks of the future."

It was in the company of Geoffrey Sergeant and Professor Angus and their friends, men who followed a high Christian tradition, and cherished him and believed in him, that John completed his contribution to the Rugby poetry competition. The poem, "Brave New World", was intended, he explained in a brief "Author's Note", "to portray, with the assistance of Three Voices (supposed to represent Disillusionment, the voices of the Dead, and a chorus of Angels) the Aspirations, Disillusionment and subsequent Re-encouragement of a central figure I have called Youth." The poem, though involved and abstruse, is full of solid thought, and has touches of authentic magic.

>   ". . . the sad,
>   Long look of moonlight"

is something to remember, and a war-ridden generation is not likely to forget

> "The haunting drift of death in the somber wind."

The most sustained passage in the poem is a sonnet spoken by "the Dead", which John subsequently reprinted with some changes in his little volume, under the title "Song of the Dead—a Reproach to This Century":

"*Also our lives were tragic; we believed*
In the earth, heavy beneath us, trusted the sun
As it played on leaves and flowers, and we conceived
Truth, and True Beauty,—End of Things Begun;
We, too, have laughed, and sung our hundred songs.
The sons we bore were perfect in our eyes.
We called them Brave, Original, and Wise;
We saw them slain, with faith we bore our wrongs,
—Longed, too, for happiness; and knew despair,
Lay with our dreams in the gutters and were deceived
By eyes of women; whispered hand in hand—
And loved the moonlight on a lover's hair.
We were but a day in Eternity,—yet we believed" . . .

Other poets, at sixteen, might have found difficulty in holding a long dialogue between Truth, the Dead and the Disillusioned at that level, and the poem has its arid stretches before and after the Angels descend to lead Youth abruptly and almost by main force to the sunlit heights of faith.

Throughout, there are lines of genuine perception and beauty. The Dead implore Youth to seek the meaning of life while there is yet time,

"*For after death it is too late to discover*
The secret that the living must unveil.
You cannot dig men's hearts up from the dust

And think to tell their secrets from their bones.
You cannot stare between their eyepits, thinking
To solve the riddle of Eternity. . . ."

Youth's cry,

"What hope is there that I shall live again"

sounds strangely fresh for all the millennia since it first broke
from the parched lips of Job.

Youth is not convinced when the Angels speak of God.

"Can he give me dawn-light at evening? Can the
Twilight of my hopes be turned to morning?"—

pointing out that

"Great minds have sought him . . . lacking someone else.
He has always been second, pitiful,
A god who's always taken second place,
That might prove useful, and yet never proves. . . ."

But the Angels convince him, though the final word is of
a blind rather than of a seeing faith:

"Cease doubting what is shadow, what is flesh.
What matters it to you, except that God
Has pierced your stubborn heart . . . and come alive?"

The fact was that, for John himself, God hadn't. The
obdurate heart was still unpierced. The struggle had actually not yet begun.

6

"The long, familiar faces", to which he had referred in one of his sonnets, beamed on Johnny Magee for three of his four years at Rugby, but, towards the end of his fourth year, the frowns came. Something happened; no one knew quite what; possibly he did not know himself. Perhaps love frowned before the brows of the teachers contracted, but the evidence is otherwise. The reasons for the decline of his interest in getting himself educated were, in fact, complex, as complex as the troubled heart of adolescent youth. But, whatever the reasons, his grades went on a toboggan, others aspired to first place in the form and he offered them no competition. Johnny warned his family that his report would be "stinking", but next year he would go out for a scholarship. "What I have been doing this term," he remarked with a breadth of candor which only a boy could encompass, "is to try and reconcile myself to the higher standard of work necessary for any thought of a scholarship without plunging right into the thick of it."

That was just about what it was. The report proved as disturbing to the nostrils as he had expected: *Scripture*—"His written work shows that he more readily expounds his own view than seeks to understand his author's." *English*—"Probably the most able boy in the form, so far as written work is concerned, but certainly not the most industrious." *Aristophanes*—"Very poor recently. He struggles, or appears to, with little result." The French teacher described him as "capable and voluble but careless". Another master pointed out that he had been "deliberately idle for reasons with which I cannot sympathize, although he has been perfectly honest and frank in explaining them."

Two years later, in a letter to his mother, Johnny revealed the philosophic background, such as it was, of his debacle. "I had for some time been a little dissatisfied with the system at Rugby, whereby everyone worked for material reward, whether it be in the shape of a prize for good work, or a high mark, or a move into the next form. That seemed to me wrong, so, in true Faustian spirit, I decided to renounce that system and work for what I considered to be my own good, without regard for the competition of others. Of course, if I had known it was to be my last term there, I would not have done it; and it was not a very great success; but I feel that I profited by the experiment."

The explanation had a noble ring, and Johnny was not above magniloquence. The real truth was that he was in that most trying stage of a boy's growth—trying to himself and others—when he was beginning to feel his oats, intellectually.

The spring vacation—the talk, the contact with mature minds, the experience of being listened to and treated as an equal by grown men; above all the friendship, even the admiration of a man as mature and as sensitive as Geoffrey Sergeant—had been the high-point, to that moment, of John's life, and shook him a little off his balance. Unduly shy at the beginning of the excursion, at the prospect of being with young men so much older than himself, his sense of inferiority had changed to self-esteem when he found that he could hold his own. Finding his opinions taken seriously by scholars of men's estate, he persuaded himself that he himself was, to all intents and purposes, a man, in brains the equal, if not the superior, of most of the adults he met.

After the stimulating interlude, the School seemed to him crude, materially minded and intolerant. He told the headmaster so. Hugh Lyon—Johnny had a way of calling him by his first name—was inclined to agree; it was true, the School was all these things. But wasn't it the part of wisdom to be tolerant himself and appreciate all that he himself still had to learn? And might it not be well for him to subordinate himself to a discipline which, in the long run, could do him nothing but good? A little more humility, perhaps, a little more endurance. . . .

Johnny was not at an age at which humility seems attractive. He raged, feeling that rage was noble, striking out blindly in an effort to reduce his schoolmates and his teachers to what appeared to his jaundiced eye their true proportions. In a satire, "provoked by Sunday Chapel at Rugby", and inspired by Alexander Pope, he painted his fellows.

"But who are these who enter one by one
The darkened halls, their passive labours done?
Who these black minions, though with Youth endowed,
Who file within, a pale plebian crowd?
Are these the servants of a loftier race?
And why this torpid stare on every face? . . ."

Then the masters—

"Oh, blind, unseeing fools, who seek Control,
Who think to crush from Youth his very soul;

Who saturate his mind with wisdom trite
And turn his aspirations into blight. . . ."

The headmaster, loving the boy, seeing the poet in him
unfold, saw what others missed, that the trouble with Johnny's grades was mainly that Johnny was growing up. "He
was growing up fast," he pointed out later, "faster than his
contemporaries, and began to find the rules and con-
ventions of a Public School uncongenial." "The Head"
squelched him when he was self-assertive and did what he
could to blast his self-absorption. Johnny's very hunger to
do the right thing defeated his mentor, since each high-
stepping ego-strut would be succeeded by a fit of remorse
and the very extreme of self-depreciation. "This makes it
hard for anyone to talk to him too severely," Lyon pointed
out to Mrs. Magee. "These sensitive yet opinionated young
men are frightfully hard to handle, and I feel I have not
made much of a success of it."

The trouble was that Johnny's emotional life had not
caught up with his brains. He had a man's intelligence, but
his emotional life was still that of the child. Once, that
year, when he was alone with his father, he suddenly burst
into tears. His father could not make out what was troubling
him, though the name which slipped from his lips suggested
a tiff with the fair Diana. John was not only self-centered
but self-willed. He wanted his own way and, figuratively
speaking, kicked and screamed when he couldn't get it. He
groused, he sulked. He walked, like Kipling's cat, "by his
wild lones".

He was perplexed by the wonder and terror of life, conscious of dark powers in him and around him, exalted one

moment, depressed the next, torn between God and the
Devil, and worshipfully in love. At the conclusion of a visit
to the Lyons in Yorkshire the previous summer, Robin
Hood's Bay had been the background of one episode of
the Diana-idyll.

> "If, when we walked together in the rain,
> While tears and raindrops mingled in our eyes;
> And talked of foolish things, to ease the pain
> Of parting; when we thought we could disguise
> Our feelings in the light of stolen joy;
> When fawning bracken kissed our sodden shoes,
> And hand in hand, determined to enjoy
> Those last few moments we were soon to lose,
> We walked in silence, awed by shrouding mist
> And wondered at that silent wilderness
> Of moor and mountain, and the pall above,
> And laughed awhile,—and sometimes all but kissed;
> If then we found a little happiness,
> Did neither of us see that this was . . . Love?"

With Diana he was tender, with Hugh Lyon disciplined,
but in vacations at Foxburrow, the Magee home on the
Channel in Kent, not far from Dover, he could be madden-
ing. High-strung like all the Magees, there were days when
he made no effort to fit himself into the family life. He
"high-hatted" his brothers—all younger than himself—and
was inclined to be generally patronizing, convinced that his
own opinion was sounder than his father's, even in matters
of Biblical exegesis. His father—being a Christian, sitting on
the volcanic temper of the Scotch-Irish Magees—had a trying time of it.

Johnny himself knew he was often no comfort in a home. "I know I'm simply frightful at times," he wrote his parents, "but I don't really mean to be. I know I tend to live for my own enjoyment, but I think I'm being quite truthful that I don't do this just for the sake of enjoyment itself. It's just like drugging myself. I find life frightfully depressing at times and I simply *have* to get my thoughts away into the skies. That's why I suddenly rush off at unearthly hours to the cinema, to the sea, up on the downs with my gun, to see a friend. I have to find an outlet for my emotions. When I get like that, I just haven't the power to be nice to anyone; I immediately retire into my shell, put out my bristles, and shun the company of men.

"I think it's partly because at home I've no one of my own age, who is at all of my temperament or who can understand me. And I have to have such people. That's why I'm often happier at school than I am at home. It's not that I don't like home, because I do. But there is, and always will be, a gap where I need a friend of my own age. Believe me, I'm not really as sour as I appear to be. I can be very unselfish and thoughtful, but I don't get on with many people and the few that I do get on well with aren't always available at the right moments.

"Please don't think that I don't love you both, my dears, because I do, ever so much, though I make you both very unhappy sometimes. I don't fit in at home, simply because my mind, if you like, works differently from yours, and I just can't understand your point of view any more than you can see mine. Perhaps one day I shall be able to leave my shell behind me and take my allotted place in life. However, at the moment, I have got a pretty heavy weight on my heart, and I just can't do without friends who can understand my point of view, who can show genuine sympathy.

"I wish I could express all this better. I'm making an awful hash of it, but please don't misunderstand more than necessary. When I say that I don't fit into the home I don't cast any aspersions *at all* on home, or you; I simply mean that I regard life in a different way from you two, though probably (in fact, certainly) an inferior one."

When, after a Christmas vacation, which left the household strewn as it were with wreckage, his father and mother wrote him a letter pointing out how abominably he had disported himself, his penitence made up for much. "One never realizes these things until afterwards," he replied. "Retrospection seems to paint one's sins in a much more lurid hue than that in which they appeared at the time. I really can't understand why I've been so utterly beastly to you all."

They wouldn't, he was sure, believe that his remorse was genuine, but there was no harm in his pointing out that he was in a passing phase. "During the past year I have had more emotional upsets than most people of my age. My soul is a soul at war with itself—and certainly not at peace with God."

He poured out to his father and mother all the emotional bewilderment of the boy of sixteen, with a gift of expression granted to few of that age. "I am selfish, I know, but I loathe myself for my self-centeredness. I have had long talks with several friends of mine here and have concluded that everybody of my age feels similar sentiments about his home. It is an age of dissatisfaction and ambitions, conflicting ideals, etc., which all makes things rather difficult. That is not an *excuse*—it is a genuine attempt to account for something which I can't explain any other way." So, he added, he was going to stay away from "the family" for a while, spending his next vacation with friends, and trusted that the family would feel neither too much regret nor too much relief.

His troubles with his family were symptomatic of an undeveloped social sense, characteristic of brainy or aesthetic boys with a highly developed emotional nature. He had failed as a monitor at St. Clare, proving unwilling to take responsibility, and he had failed no less as a prefect at Rugby. He did some work as an editor of the school magazine, the *New Rugbeian*, but that, after all, was in line with his dearest predilections. The "glimpses" of what he might do for the common life of the School, of which he had written wistfully to his mother, never evolved into action. Like most sons of the uneasy Thirties, moreover, he looked with a cynical eye on patriotism, and found a refuge from responsibility in a strongly individualistic pacifism, not unmixed with self-righteousness.

7

He found it in the vacation which was to testify to his independence of his family, that same vacation which had proved so upsetting to his equilibrium as a school-boy.

More clearly than the statesmen of the day, he realized that war was inevitable, and, in that Spring of 1939, said so in his Rugby poem:

"Men's fates are already set.
There is no need of asking fortune-tellers.
They will have brought this evil on themselves.
For here are a million people, surly with traffic,
Each with his hereditary power of instability,
Each on his way to become a commercial corsair,
Each with his fill of hollow aspirations,
Competing with one another in the tawdry
Glitter and speed of machines—mechanical mania—
Unable in the supervening blankness
Of middle age to sift the good from evil,
Taking it all as one—
                          their only dread
Unpopularity and social inconsequence . . .
These need a cleansing, some all-purging tempest
To shake the stagnant pool of their convictions,
Leaving with them fresh hopes, as after a night-mare,
For then the strange night-wonder will be upon them.
These will stare as dream-awakened men in wonder. . . ."

In the face of a conflict, which appeared inevitable, what, Geoffrey and John had queried, is the duty of the Christian? What is the extent of Christian neighborliness? Does Christianity, they had asked, deny the local and exclusive, the partial form of loyalty such as patriotism? To the query, What, in this world-wide condition could one individual do? —Professor Angus, their host, had pointed out that "Christians exist to attempt what the world considers impossible."

"We agreed," Geoffrey wrote later, "that, although warfare may apparently defend a particular and relatively good form of government, and may deflect evil, as perhaps it did in the first World War, it certainly does not overcome it. In other words, for Christians, all war is civil war. We knew, of course, that these were very exalted and absolute ideals, and that, in terms of purely human wisdom, it may be necessary to advance by less radical standards."

John's sensitive spirit, inclined to reach out for the highest he could discern, came out of his experience with Geoffrey, at Mortehoe, convinced that war was inconsistent with the Christian principles in which he had been confirmed. John took his Christian faith seriously. It meant something to him. A part of the adolescent paradox that he was, was that he could be almost unbearable in his relations with others, and yet be devout, that, as the headmaster of St. Clare had noted, before he was in his teens, he could movingly read the Lesson in Chapel and, at the next moment, "have to have a lesson read to him."

He wrote his mother that he had become an outright pacifist. "That's what Jesus would have wanted."

His mother shuddered. Her father's father and brother had both been colonels of British regiments in India. Her own brothers were in the army. To offer your life for King and Country seemed to her not the denial of Christ, as the pacifist claimed, but the ultimate expression of devotion to Him whose symbol was the Cross. Shaken as she was by what seemed to her a form of genuine heresy, she withheld her arguments, contenting herself with forwarding John's letter to her husband in China. He would know, she wrote him, how to answer it.

He did, choosing as always the way of understanding and toleration, making no effort to shake his son's convictions, though he could not share them. He was himself in the very midst of a vast battlefield, having remained in Nanking during and after the siege, and risked his life as a member of the International Safety Zone Commission, doing what he could to protect women from outrage, and, with his amateur motion-picture camera, to collect evidence which might help the western world see how Japan made war.

He himself loathed war, he wrote John, but there were things even worse than war. If Japan triumphed, China would be flooded with narcotics, and the Chinese people would go to pieces physically and morally. On the other hand, he had seen what the defense of their country had done to revitalize and uplift that same people. So, though he offered no generalizations on war as a moral agent, he could not, in this specific instance, himself be a pacifist.

Johnny was impressed. The war of nerves, sending its cohorts along the ether even into the sheltered quiet of Rugby, did its part to bring him to the admission that "complete pacifism is not what is meant for me."

He went to Bisley for rifle practice, not without a feeling of guilt, and wrote to Geoffrey, referring to the collision between the exclusive claims of patriotism and the universal ideal of Christianity. "I went to see a hair-raising film called 'Dawn Patrol'," he added, "and came out subconsciously determined to be an airman—in fact I all but enlisted. On reflection, however, I recall our talks at Mortehoe, and remain a civilian!"

His newly found pacifism died hard. A chill passed over him when the English papers began to discuss the age limit of seventeen for the draft! He was almost that age! "It makes me all but physically sick to think that, at the behest of one man, I may have to Surrender my Life to God and my Country, Die for my King, or whatever the up-to-date term is. What a lot of bogus romanticism there is about War! Romanticism ceases to be what it is, in terms of Mud and Bullets!"

He poured his terror into verse.

> "I thought to find
> Glory, fighting
> Long struggles with men,
> With one man smiting
> Another; the soldier-pain
> Of effort; that after
> There would be rest—and laughter.
>
> "But what I found was
> Mangled men, biting
> A heathen dust, and ground
> Strewn with heads and
> Eyes and twisted hands

Holding nothing.
God! Why is it that no one understands
The meaning of
FUTILITY?
They would, had they but seen
Horrible, staring eyes. . . ."

He found that his housemates at Rugby were tortured like himself by the prospect opening before them. Meeting, evenings, in one of the studies, ostensibly to read Virgil or Aristophanes, they talked "the evening out (and very often the morning in)" asking what they would do if war should come. Their answer had the cynicism of a vast inexperience. If they could find "a suitable victim", they would marry—"a marriage of mutual compromise"—whatever that might mean—rather than a life-time union, without too much sentiment on the part of the male, or too many regrets, if the male were killed, on the feminine side. "I wonder," he wrote, "if boys talked the same way before the last War?"

Johnny, really shaken, dodged the day's news, and shocked his mother in August of the fateful year, 1939, by telling her that he had not looked at a newspaper in months. He seemed to be living in a dream-world of his own, completely detached from the thunder-laden reality. "I'm much happier than you are," he told her. "You read about the tense situation in the world and are troubled by it. I live in blissful ignorance of it, which is much more sensible."

"I'm not doing a stroke of work this term," he wrote Geoffrey Sergeant. "It feels grand, so exhilarating. What's the use of working, waiting for the 'gun-butt'? Why shouldn't I enjoy myself while I can?"

And, after all, he ended the year in glory, for "Brave New World" won the poetry prize, the prize which, thirty-four years before, had been won by his hero, Rupert Brooke.

8

John came to the United States, in the summer of 1939, with the idea of acquainting himself again with his own country, which he had not seen for five years, and returning in the autumn for his final year at Rugby. He set out with some qualms, for the family finances had suffered a setback, and tried, in fact, to persuade his father that he would like to stay in England. There was a car, he wrote, that he could buy for nine pounds sterling—a venerable but hearty veteran which ran 30 miles to the gallon, and which he would like to tour England in. "I have had an invitation up to Scotland in the summer to stay with the Lyons." He wanted to go to America, and yet, he did want to see Diana, who was with them, and the car would take him to Scotland for a song. His final argument was characteristically dramatic —and darkly prophetic. "With the world in its present precarious position, few people of my age put their chances of survival after twenty (to put it crudely) at more than about fifty-fifty, and I want to do as much as I can while I've got the opportunity."

But he was not sorry to be overruled, with the help of a generous fairy godmother, his father's sister, Mary Scaife, in Pittsburgh, who felt that John was expatriating himself —a process with which Americans have always been unsympathetic except as it applies to the alien in the United States—and had better get to know his own country before he lost contact with it altogether. John came by the

Queen Mary, but third class, falling in with a party of some forty American music-teachers, including a number of girls, very young and very enticing. "I never knew the Atlantic could be so lovely," John chanted, in a letter to his father.

There was a Girl from Georgia who made the Atlantic more and more entrancing as the voyage proceeded, but, by the time the vessel was approaching the American shore, she had been supplanted by a Girl from Colorado. John wrote his father about it with disarming candor. There was one memorable night of dancing in the third class until the band went to bed, and dancing in the tourist cabin until that band too folded up, then back to the third for more dancing, with the nimble-fingered young ladies successively at the piano, and then the boat-deck to see the dawn in. There was happily a moon to keep the three boys and three girls occupied until the sun took over. "The girl I was with was extremely pleasant," John wrote, which is evident from what follows. "We got very sentimental, and almost began to weep because it was the last time we should ever watch the sun in together again!" Yet, he added, it had been one of the happiest times of his life. "It will probably sound all very sordid to you, but you would change your mind, I know, if you had met the girls in question. I only wish you could have been there too," he added, his sense of humor for once deserting him, "as I know you would have loved it, though it was so sad." One ventures to suggest that the one who really should have been there was Mr. Booth Tarkington, making notes for a new episode in the career of William Sylvanus Baxter.

"Ordinarily," John points out sagely, "a party of young

people necking in the moonlight is apt to lead to complications of varying degree, but there was not a suggestion of anything like that."

John was, in fact, rather surprised, he wrote his father, that there wasn't. His inquiring mind and his philosophic bent combined to make him wonder about it even while he held the lovely creature in his arms. "It dawned on me then that sex can be a very beautiful thing if kept in its proper place and not allowed to run out of hand."

The sunrise, under the circumstances, was necessarily "inexpressibly wonderful." It was only when the other passengers, coming on deck at breakfast-time, began to eye the young pair "with various expressions of amusement", that John realized that he was still wearing his dinner jacket.

At the Grand Central Station in New York that day there were tearful farewells. "Of course, the bottom seemed to have fallen out of a world which had, for me, suddenly become intensely lovely."

The bottom, it happened, was promptly restored, and, a week later, visiting friends of the Magee family at Vineyard Haven, John noted to his surprise, after an evening under the same moon with a different girl, that his coat and face were covered with lipstick.

His love appeared to be as constant as any romanticist might desire; it was only its object that varied.

He saw it all clearly enough.

"*Always there will be loves that drift, as ours;*
Beautiful faces, touched by fresher winds
Change suddenly;—and soon are blown away;

Passion forgets her few, ecstatic hours
Soon after, in new hearts, and other minds,
—And finds enchantment for another day!"

The visit on Martha's Vineyard was brief, and toward the end of August, John found himself established in his Aunt Mary's comfortable apartment in Pittsburgh, making such contact as his surroundings provided with the ideals and the way of life of his own country. The experience proved intoxicating.

The Magees had been among the early settlers of the robustious town where the rivers meet, and had grown up with the dynamic, smoke-stained city. An early Magee had been the first elected officer of the county. His son discreetly married the daughter of "Granny" Hogg, a great character in Pittsburgh's early days, who died, rich in real estate, at the age of one hundred and ten! John's great-uncle Christopher, the famous "Chris" Magee of Pennsylvania politics, had been president of the Pittsburgh street railways, and, with the redoubtable William Flinn, ruled the political life of Allegheny County. Most of the Magees had had brains, personal magnetism and a flair for politics; a few had had a large thirst. Through the Gillespies, a genuine artistic strain entered the Magee tribe, rarer than intelligence, political dexterity or a taste for liquor in Pittsburgh's early days, and responsible for the first art store in the city and the leading musical society. The Magee quality held up through successive generations, both in its energy and its charm. One of young John's first cousins, Alan Scaife, was, at forty, chairman of the board of directors of the largest coal company in the world; his brother Verner, president of one of the oldest steel plants in the city. Another cousin, Edward Magee, son of John's Uncle Jim, was working in an Oregon lumber camp, and would be in a flying fortress over Java soon after John began to mix with Messerschmitts over the English Channel.

The Magees were of the world of industry and the social game, and, after thirty years, were still wondering how one of them could so far have forgotten himself and his background as to become a Christian missionary. The clan was loyal to its own, and devoted to the elder John, who had been converted as a school-boy at Hotchkiss, but inclined to think that a little China was enough, if not too much, feeling that he should bring his family home and rear his sons in the Pittsburgh tradition.

They welcomed his eldest with open arms. Johnny had lived in Pittsburgh when he was twelve, knew them all and, in a sense, was coming home. He had great charm when he wanted to exercise it, and this time he stretched himself. All the doors flew open, his aunt put him up at the Rolling Rock Club—40,000 acres of it—and the girls fluttered and succumbed. It was wholly characteristic of him that, shortly after his arrival, having learned the latest dance-steps out of a manual, he and his partner, at his first party, won the prize for the best dancing.

For a while Johnny was in heaven. He had never seen so many girls at one time, or any, in fact, so "got up" to entrance the unwary. English girls were lovely—none lovelier than Diana—but they didn't dress or manage their hair or paint their cheeks and lips like these bewildering sub-debs. Johnny took one look at the little Venuses, born of the foam, and went off the deep end.

His hospitable and devoted Aunt Mary, "my wonderful Aunt Mary", as he called her, scarcely saw him. He was driving or riding all day, dancing or skylarking most of the night. "One thing I have noticed—rather painfully—is," he wrote his father, "that this country never goes to bed at all, so no wonder it (and I) are so seldom up for breakfast."

Now and then he came to a meal, and he didn't bother to say in advance when that might or might not be. His aunt, his uncle, and other members of the circle of elders were first hurt, then indignant. Their indignation rose to siren-pitch when the bill from the Country Club came in. Johnny, in his innocence, had not realized that everything did not go with the privileges of a guest-card. He was convincingly penitent. "I have never lived the life of the American aristocrat before," he reminded his mother, when the repercussions began to make themselves felt, "and, when plunged into it, I completely lost my bearings. . . . For instance, at Rolling Rock, some people would ask me to go riding with them. Why, of course, I went riding. There would be a hunt. Of course, I would go hunting, if possible—and it was, so I did. But I had not the remotest idea that each time I rode it was adding $5 to Aunt Mary's bill. . . . Naturally I tried to avoid extravagance, but, even so, the money rolled out of my pockets almost before I knew it was in them."

The outbreak of the war in Europe complicated a situation which already was complex enough. England's peril deepened John's love for the country in which he had spent his happy, growing years. He had, moreover, promised his pacifist friends that, in case war came, he would join the Pacifist Service Corps, and though, under the impact of

war, his pacifism was wearing thin, his promise was a good
excuse to get back to England. He besieged the State Department for a passport, pulling every wire he saw dangling
anywhere, all in vain.

He spent money more irresponsibly than ever. It was
partly, of course, he explained to his father two months
later when the fever had subsided, that he was trying to
keep up with "a pretty fast set to whom money was nothing," but, he admitted, there was more to his extravagance
than that. He had been "under intense emotional strain",
and "terribly homesick", giving himself to despondent reflection on England, "which could only be dispelled by
parties and 'dates', etc., which, of course, cost money. I
realize now that this was a cowardly and selfish policy to
adopt, but at the time I was just fleeing from a Reality
which pointed its finger at me, threatening exile in a strange
(for such it is!) land for the duration of hostilities, which
meant—what? Two? Four? Six years? But that's the penalty,
I suppose, for having imagination! Unknown to Aunt Mary
and Uncle Jim, I spent two weeks looking for a job in
Pittsburgh, but no one seemed to want a stranger with no
references or commercial training of any kind. I knew that,
if I once settled down to a job, it would be something to
take my mind off the future, and something tangibly creative—financially speaking, at any rate."

When John, raw from the scoldings for his spending-
spree, told his Pittsburgh relatives of his determination to
go to work, the effect was other than he expected.

He announced his decision possibly a little more gran-
diloquently than he intended, and his father's brother blew
up. John had no real wish to help the family out, now,

honestly, did he? He had been just talking, hadn't he? Johnny agreed that he had perhaps lost his head and said a good deal about "high ideals", which was "to a certain degree insincere and exaggerated." He had been told before that he was an exhibitionist, that he dramatized life too much and never came down to reality, and perhaps it was true. But he *was* ready to take a job, even as a soda-jerker, if necessary, in order to feel that he was, to some small extent, helping to ease the financial tension.

"I imagine you have had no difficulty in believing in yourself," he wrote the affronted uncle, who was actually a very warm-hearted man, with many of John's own characteristics. "Well, I find immense difficulty in having any faith whatsoever in myself. It has led me to much introspection, which has made me more or less of an introvert, and has had the effect of making me extremely self-centered. Add to that a deep desire to do crazy things to escape convention; and you have the picture . . . a picture with much room for improvement, I will admit, but not, I think, quite as insincere as you seem anxious to indicate."

With the idea of a job in the ash-can, what was he to do? The aunts and uncles were convinced he should go back to school, to an American school, since Rugby was out of the question, get the final credits he needed and follow the Magee tradition to Yale. The Avon School, near Hartford, to which his long-suffering and continuously generous Aunt Mary applied, agreed to make a place for him.

9

Conscious of family disapproval—not only in Pittsburgh but in England, where his mother's brothers were joining his American uncles in shocked reprobation—in a "mental turmoil", as he wrote his mother, unsure of himself, aching to be in Britain to take what came in the company of his family and his friends, John took up again the labors of a school-boy.

Outwardly, Avon was everything to make him feel at home, for its architecture was Tudor English and romantic. The low brick buildings were

"Bowered deep in tufted trees,"

like the ancient English villages he loved, and looked over a valley that might have been in the Cotswolds.

"This is, topographically, a grand place," John wrote his father. "There is riding, shooting, fishing, polo, hunting, beagling—everything a man could want."

As a place to steady his over-excited nerves and emotions, torn by the war and the separation from his friends, while, from the creative thinking of the past, he gained perspective in the present, Avon was possibly as satisfactory as any American school would have been. Like John himself, it was in transition. It would, a year or two later, find a new base, a more solid foundation of principle and leadership. Meanwhile, it had the solid assets of an exceptional faculty, a charming setting and the priceless tradition that manual labor of some sort must go with the training of the mind.

Academically, John wrote his father, a little patronizingly, the school would do well enough. But there was little Latin and no Greek at all, and what would happen to his classics? "It's a great throwback; but I realize nothing can be done about it." He had neither the background nor the interest for substantial work in mathematics or science, and once more drank deep of literature and philosophy.

The serene and cultivated teacher of art, Paul Child, himself a gifted worker in the graphic arts, went out of his way to look up "the new English boy" and ask him to drop in to his quarters for tea.

John's face lit up. "Oh, tea! I certainly will." There was a song he liked to sing, "Everything Stops for Tea."

Several boys were already in the master's room when he arrived. "John, with his aura of sophistication and charm," Child wrote later, "was rather like a cockatoo in a cage full of pigeons. He looked at everything—pictures, books, furniture, and the other young men—with an unabashed interest. It was apparent at once that he was sensitive, intelligent, and perhaps even a little priggish. We fell almost at once into a discussion of modern poetry, with the pigeons flapping rather feebly behind, and, when he left, he borrowed a volume of Lorca's poems which had just been published. Subsequently he read other books from my library, such things as 'High Wind in Jamaica', several of Ezra Pound's essays, Kenneth Patchen's 'First Will and Testament', E. E. Cummings' 'The Enormous Room', and a series of excerpts from the work of Henry Miller.

"In discussing these books he showed unusual grasp of the aesthetic intentions of the writers, but his other critical attitudes seemed somewhat colored by a determined 'English', and also by the fact that he simply hadn't lived long enough to have sensed the worth of different strata of society. His own background was quite naturally the touchstone against which he tried all new experiences, new impressions, new foods and new attitudes."

The teacher of art was only one of several on the faculty who kept John's mind humming. "The Sixth Form course in English was organized for the purpose of making young men *think*, with as much exciting conflict in ideas as possible," wrote the English master, Francis H. Bangs, son of that John Kendrick Bangs whose humor had entranced an earlier, less sophisticated generation, and whose integrity had cost him his editorship of a leading weekly. The teacher noted in John Magee's mind "an intellectual athleticism quite remarkable. He dealt with ideas with a gay ease. His mind worked lyrically and mountingly. He was fascinated by the Socratic dialectic and did not leave off at the end of a Platonic dialogue but continued the process himself." The teacher lifted the seventeen-year-old boy to a perilous notoriety when he broadcast through the school that a theme he had written about Plato's *Symposium* "would get the writer into any American university at this minute." John heard himself described as "the most intelligent person who had ever come to the school," and ruefully commented to his father on the difficulty he expected to have in living up to such praise.

Avon was outstanding among American schools in its development of student self-government, but John, untrained in political thinking, missed the point completely, merely resenting a system which placed classmates, whom he regarded as inferior in intellect and culture, in authority over him in matters concerning dress and dormitory life. The boys soon found it impractical to prosecute him, since his suavity and wit under fire had a tendency to make monkeys of his judges, and they developed extra-legal methods of discipline to which he developed extra-legal responses. But when a posse forcibly cut the hair of a youth who had failed to visit the barber, John, at a school meeting, upheld the cause of democracy in a defense of the freedom of the individual to wear his hair as long as he wanted.

He found all this amusing enough, but childish, and got away when he could, to New York or elsewhere for weekends, to see one or another of a string of girls who had captivated his impressionable affections. "One thing America is doing to me," he wrote his mother. "Its womanhood has cut me up so many times that each new experience is somewhat nullified by the last; and I like to think of myself as becoming more sober and moderate when emotionally aroused. However, this may be imagination."

It was a poor tribute to his country. The fact was, he was disappointed in this America that his father had told him about, and a little heartsick in his disillusionment. The worldliness of the American scene—the great houses, the high-powered cars, the country clubs, the pretty girls and boys, with no thought beyond fast driving and cocktails and dancing and sex— This was America, was it? At the school, "the affluent morons", chattering about athletics and cars and girls, girls and cars and athletics, with never an aspiration beyond, or apparently any idea that there *was* anything beyond—this, too, was America, was it?

The worldliness allured him. The artist in him loved the

fine houses, the luxury, the soft beauty of the women; the common clay in him enjoyed the let-down of it, the sense that he could be as self-indulgent as he had always wanted to be and it was all right, everybody was doing it and he was a fool not to run with the crowd. But all that was fine in him rebelled.

·"There is no poetry, no imagination, no *feeling*, in this country, Geoff!" he wailed to his Cambridge friend, with the sweeping finality of seventeen. "It is hard and organized. Here Virtue is the number of cars a man has, and Religion is Money. No one can amuse himself without vast expenditure, and then only for a transient 'kick'. The brothels are full everywhere (mostly with 18-year olds) and countless people are arrested for drunkenness in the big cities daily. To these it is fantastic that a man can find ecstasy (as we did!) walking with nothing but a stick and sixpence in our pockets in the face of the freshening wind over some southern down."

No one apparently told Johnny Magee that the luxury and the self-indulgence which he bewailed were only a part of this America he was seeing as an adult for the first time, a blatant part, heavily advertised in the movies and the magazines, but only a part, even a small part; that, in Pittsburgh itself, in the great plants sending steel across the sea for the defense of the England he loved, was another America, grimy, sweat-stained and hard-working; that, among the green slopes east and west of the junction of the great rivers, was still another America, hard-working, too, and free-hearted; and, in the Great Valley between the Alleghenies and the Rockies, still another; and beyond the Rockies, yet one more; a nation and a people, seeing a great hope for themselves and for all mankind, and ready to die, if necessary, to keep that hope alive.

But no one showed him that America. He was conscious only of the hardness and materialism—which America's own most penetrating minds were lamenting—and, under it, a profound dissatisfaction with life, "which exists all over America, believe me," he wrote his mother. "I haven't, as you say, met an awful lot of Americans, but I have met a fairly good cross-section of American life without finding an exception yet."

The America he saw was for him exile. "Sometimes," he wrote his mother, "I wake up in the morning quite prepared to believe that this has all been a great nightmare—though with its more pleasant moments—but before long I realize that the oaken walls of my little room at Avon are *not*, as I had at first imagined, the panelled walls of the oak-room at Foxburrow (dear place!) and that David will *not* burst excitedly at any moment into my room with news of a favoring wind and tide for sailing!

"The fact of Reality hits me periodically like a brickbat, and I feel that everything that ever meant anything to me is but a dead and lifeless memory. I wonder if I'm the most ghastly sentimentalist, or whether I am being given the ability to see that England meant life and feeling to me?

"In your letter, you referred to a letter of mine in which I made the rather sweeping statement 'that there is no poetry in Americans,' but I cannot help feeling that I was right, at least in part, in so far as I interpreted the word 'poetry' as meaning enthusiasm, feeling,—in fact, the very breath of life! I don't want to be melodramatic, mother, but something in me is dying, irrevocably, irretrievably; I am beginning simply to *exist*, whereas before, at any rate at moments, I *lived*."

Had he been discontented during his last year at Rugby? Already in England he had been "jealous of the wealthy and frivolous of which I had heard so much, yet knew so little. In moments like this I realize, deep down, that I have had my fill of it. Yet there is a sort of futility in trying to escape from the demands of its existence. To get away from it all, to walk again on the beach at Kingsdown, and feel the freshening wind on one's face, and wonder, perhaps, if there are any chocolate biscuits left for tea! There was an ecstasy there, and I was damned (in every sense of the word) into overlooking it in all my blindness.

"And now I feel a growing fear—the kind that might well bring a cold sweat to the brow, if allowed to play further on one—that, before long, it will be too late, and I shall be so enmeshed in the snare of material wanting never to be able to enjoy living for its own sake, and not for the sake of the amusement it may bring.

"Please don't tell me," he added feverishly, "that I've been making mountains out of mole-hills, because if You do, there is no one else who will understand."

In his torment he cried like a child for his mother. "I am feeling terribly homesick for you. I want to cry out to everyone here that I love you, and want to get back to your side. I think you will find me changed in some ways. I have had a good time. Now I want to see you have a good time, and I am so longing to get back to help out! I know things are twice as difficult for you as they are for me. And for that very reason I shall never be really happy over here. Don't you believe a man should live by his convictions? I am convinced my place is in England, and, if ever I see the opportunity, *I'm coming*."

10

Life brightened for him at Avon. He found a few con-
genial spirits with whom he could retreat to a hidden
cranny, to smoke and talk all evening of literature and life
and the foggy prospect for youth. He and a boy named
Phil May from Pittsburgh, and another friend, Larry Viles,
were keeping to themselves, he wrote his mother, "not from
any motive of snobbishness, but rather as a sort of Cave of
Adullam (minus the general grudge)." The self-conscious
"clique", he admitted, "has aroused not a little hostility on
the part of the more democratically minded." That was the
least of his worries. The main thing was that in this little
group, and with some of the masters, he was "finding a
certain sanity".

But his heart was in England. Writing his father, he expressed doubt whether his English education had not un-
fitted him for life in America. "This is a marvellous country,
with marvellous opportunities for money-making for such
as have either the talent or the interest. But it has no room
—and so I have discovered to my hurt—for dreamers and
poets. If I am to continue my life of philosophic discussion and writing—other than for a newspaper or journal—
I am positively convinced that England is the place for me."

Besides, he added, he had drunk the intoxicating wine
of pleasure and was not fooling himself about his ability
to take it or leave it. If he was to be in America, he would
be running around with the rich and would want money—

and the money would not be there. There was still another point, "I find this country to be far looser, with regard to morals, free thought, and language, than England ever will be; and it is hard, when daily surrounded by those who spurn religion, and use *very* free language, not to get in the habit oneself; and that is already happening to me."

No, he wanted to go back to England, to simple living and people grounded in the great traditions. He thought he ought to go to Oxford. "I may be wrong, but I can't help seeing life here as a sort of regression from everything I found at Rugby."

He poured out his soul in letters to Hugh Lyon, who was sympathetic but firm. Now that he was started in a new school, surely he would stick it out. "So, do settle down." He added a characteristic postscript. "Gosh, what a headmasterly letter! And I so much wanted it not to be!"

No admonitions, however kindly, could quench John's longing for England and, months later, it remained fresh and poignant. "I wonder if you realize," he wrote his mother, "how I feel about a return to England. . . . It's a funny thing; here in America I have everything: yet I have nothing. And it isn't that I have deliberately decided against making good in this country, but that I am just unsuited to it."

Meanwhile, with the State Department determined against his returning to England, he took life as he found it, preferably in New York or on Long Island, living in the present, letting the future go hang. It was quite characteristic that, when he wanted money to go to a "movie", he should pawn his bathrobe to pay for the ticket.

He experienced an evening's respite from the boredom

of school and conventional living, visiting his Uncle Jim's gifted daughter and her husband, happily established after the Bohemian pattern in New Haven. "I was at home at once," he wrote his father. "All evening and late into the night we sat and discussed everything from Free Love to Genetics. Suddenly I felt that I was born to the Bohemian life. I wanted to live, like them, in a shabby—almost sordid —little apartment, and be vaguely happy and think wonderful thoughts! One incident amused me very much. When it was time to put the baby to bed its pajamas could be found nowhere at all. . . . We ransacked everything from the ash-can to underneath the bath-tub, but with no success; and it was not until Mary was undressing the child that she found, to her surprise, that he still had them on! It was a delightful moment."

Pursued or pursuing, he enjoyed the girls, a bewildering bevy, constantly changing, constantly enchanting, going to their college dances, inviting them to school "proms". It was like him that, when he brought a girl to one of the school dances, it should have been the pretty Cuban whom a friend had invited, to whom he lost his heart, possibly because she owned a house in Surrey which she promised to bequeath to him.

Yet, there was a wonder which drew him more potently even than the magnetic little nymphs of America's garden of Pan.

"Frequently I am tempted to think of the beauty of women,
 Calling to mind the glad mouth, and the hair and eyes,
 Imagining that no other thing is so beautiful.
 But tonight I walked beneath a cold, white moon.

There were many trees—
             some still as Grecian marble;
Others alive; and whispering of strange deeds among the
     stars.
The moon all the while watching, and intensely wise—
And I know that there was the greater beauty."

The general laxity in regard to religion and morals which he found in America was, meanwhile, having its effect on him. Gilded youth's acceptance of self-indulgence as a divine right was a seductive music. Galahad? Wake up and come to life! John returned from one weekend in New York so exhilarated that he entertained the whole car, and was promptly given a going-over by the headmaster as a "show-off", and put "on bounds". Irate uncles forgot that they, too, had, at one time or another, been "lit" in their youth; aunts wrung their hands and wrote depressing letters to John's mother in England.

Johnny did what he could, with due penitence, to answer what he called the "remonstrative" letters, and did, on the whole, rather better than most boys would have done in his place. His parents, on their part, it is worth noting, did very much better than parents generally do in similar situations. They neither scolded him, nor condoned his offenses, nor failed to help him see himself as he was. They told him, in temperate words, wholly free of pious jargon, how his actions and attitudes appeared to them, but they did more. In a spirit, rare in its humility and self-knowledge, even among ministers of Christ, they admitted their own imperfections and turned his eyes inward to that which was imperfect in himself.

"When you were young, I used to excuse myself for my bad temper, for instance," his father wrote, "by saying to myself: 'I am sorry that I am this high-strung, agitated type. I wish I were more even-tempered, but I am simply not that type.' Often I showed my bad temper in the way I corrected you children, which had the wrong effect upon you. It took me many years before I found out that the root trouble was not that I was necessarily such a type, but my own human pride. When I told you children, or some Chinese, to do something, and it was not done, the issue became, not whether I was right or wrong, but personal anger on my part because I was not obeyed. I think that these sulky moods that you get into may have the same fundamental cause."

His mother was no less candid. Their honesty made him honest, their love kept him loving, their admissions of shortcomings gave him the sense that he too could build a man out of the self-willed child.

11

His religious views, meanwhile, were feeling the effects of the cynical scepticism which he found among both the intellectuals and the socially elect. Like most schools, and practically every college, Avon had its professional sceptic, taking pleasure in circumventing the orthodox. He admired the keen-witted youth from Rugby and, with the aim of liberating him from what seemed to the elder the shackles of cant and superstition, led him to books that might be depended upon to make the boy's inherited faith ridiculous in his eyes. Mature as he was, John was not mature enough to appreciate how tawdry the cynic's brilliant mockery was beside the selfless searching and impassioned aspiration of Geoffrey Sergeant and the vice-master of Trinity. John was snared by the cleverness, confusing religiosity with religion, historical authenticity with the deeper issues of the individual's relation to Deity; and experienced from one day to the next something like a Salvation Army conversion, in reverse.

"John was profoundly interested in philosophic and religious views of man and his relation to the universe," the sceptic wrote subsequently, "and the Goethean speculation, which *Faust* is, enchanted his mind. He was much interested in the law of persistency in one's own being amid the universe of action. He liked the idea of cosmic dynamism to be found basically in Goethe and with it the idea of strife (*streben*) within the great complex. . . . John fitted no orthodox pattern. If he was considered to be something of a rebel, it was doubtless because he thought for himself and had the integrity to act out of his thought. He enjoyed, as Emerson urges one to enjoy, an original relation with the universe. He was interested hospitably in the creeds and dogmas of others, but he did not allow them to become strait-jackets to his own honest thinking. I know that John was accused by some of being irreligious, but that was because he was interested in religion, and was not particularly interested in being sectarianized or even Christianized."

He was not merely interested in religion, he was obsessed by it. He had been confirmed in the Church of England in the middle of his Rugby course and the experience had stirred him, but discussions of Plato's *Phaedo* and Lucretius' *De Rerum Natura*, with liberal doses of Bertrand Russell thrown in, had convinced him that he was harboring a faith that was incompatible with his intelligence.

At intervals, his thoughtful and sensitive new friend Larry Viles would come to his room after the lights were out, and they would talk about religion, occasionally until four in the morning. Both had drifted away from their inherited spiritual moorings, both felt the pull of the *Erdgeist*, the exultation of the physical, of the body, of sex, of food, of the beauty of form and sound. Larry was conscious in his friend of an intellectual honesty to which conformity, for the sake of peace or ease, was the ultimate sin. Yet both recognized that faith was necessary to man. Faith and reason, reason and faith . . . how could you keep them in equilibrium to make the intelligent life?

So they questioned back and forth. There was something rare in this wistful effort of two boys to make their way towards an acceptable philosophy. At seventeen, both had already gone beyond the stage of mere revolt against their Christian background to the recognition that not Christianity or their elders but they themselves might be wrong, indeed probably were wrong. Yet to accept any philosophy, without fighting through doubt and darkness to achieve it, seemed base; as base as tearing down another's faith.

So, in the night watches, while their fellows were sleeping the iron sleep of boyhood, they groped their way towards something they could build their lives upon. There *was* a Power, call it what you might. But was it wholly good? Was it not both good and evil? And man, what was he? Was he more than a highly advanced form of plant life? And immortality? Was not continued existence after death the ultimate instance of wishful thinking? Yet Christianity demanded faith in immortality. How then could they accept Christianity? Yet, in a theme on Plato's *Phaedo*, John wrote: "Socrates goes to his death in the calm and absolute belief of life to come; and if he, the wisest of all philosophers, believed so, I would deem myself most foolish to believe otherwise." He was tossed to and fro.

"I am beginning to be a little apprehensive," John wrote his father, and the letter, he later admitted, was one of the most difficult he had ever had to write, "of the psychological conflict I see ahead between our respective philosophies."

He spoke of "certain changes in my own philosophy", which he trusted his father would accept "as being a fairly normal happening" for one of his years. "I have found myself unable to continue in the implicit faith in Christianity that I once had. . . . I have reached a stage of complete agnosticism. I am afraid it is going to hurt you a little to discover this metamorphosis for yourself. But I hope you will return the respect I have for your own philosophy, and for your strength in living up to your convictions, by not despising me for the conclusions I have come to."

To his father in China the letter, full of clever, cutting phrases, was a blow between the eyes. He responded with his accustomed moderation. If John would be honest with himself, and give himself to the best he knew, he (John's father) would have no fears for the future.

John, hearing that the family were all to meet in America shortly, wrote a second letter, expressing the hope that they might have a chance to talk over their conflicting views. "It may be that we will both decide that it would be better for me to live apart from the rest of the family to avoid indulgence in rituals in which I cannot place complete conviction."

His father gently pushed aside the boy's fear of conflict between them. "You can rest your heart on that score." He would respect John's views and difficulties, "and neither Mother nor I would want to embarrass you. We shall of course have family prayers, but, if these should be an embarrassment to you, you need not attend. If you ever were present, you could at least be a true agnostic and concede that we might be right, even though you could not believe with us."

They left it at that, except for John, assiduously preparing himself for a knock-down-and-drag-out argument with his father by reading Georg Brandes' "Jesus, a Myth", and dipping into various books on comparative religion.

12

John was not happy at Avon, though he managed to maintain an appearance of carefree gaiety. He might, indeed, not have been happy anywhere in America that winter, and had, in fact, been anything but happy during his last term at Rugby. But he felt strange among his American contemporaries, who regarded him, with his love of poetry and his unorthodox views of American life and purposes, definitely an exotic. With restrained irony, the school annual for 1940 speaks of his coming from Rugby "with refreshing thoughts and effervescent Anglican vitality, exerting his poetic personality to the nth degree. John has many ambitions," the annual records, "and, if we may quote them, one of them is to follow in the footsteps of Beauty, whether they lead to Gaugin, Rupert Brooke, or Mrs. Keep." Mrs. Keep was the headmistress of a fashionable school for girls, at Farmington, nearby, a place of frequent pilgrimage for John. "His principal activities," the annual goes on, "are sleeping, thinking and commenting on the oddities of school existence."

What John thought of his schoolmates he stated in a letter to his mother in no uncertain terms. Was he "unduly caustic", he asked, when he described them as "excessively characterless and unintelligent"? "I assure you that the manners, language and lack of self-control and any sort of self-respect would, in my opinion, ill become a lot of urchins in Notting Hill."

One can hear Hugh Lyon protesting at his ear: "A little more tolerance, Johnny!" John could not know that, within two years, one after another of these "characterless" youths would be clamoring for the privilege of offering his life for his country.

His mature, and, at the moment, snobbish mind, revolting against what seemed to him the "debased intellectual level", on which the rest of the boys seemed to be content to live, sought out the masters, drifting into their rooms to drink tea and talk philosophy, religion and girls, poetry and Rupert Brooke.

It was to the art teacher that he poured out his inner confusion. "It became clear, as his confidence in me grew," Child wrote subsequently, "that he felt in some measure restricted and unsupported by the American scene. His judgments of Americans and their lives were colored by a limited number of experiences which made him unaware of many categories, and, perhaps more than most young men, he seemed to suffer from the split between an intense inner life, arranged around his own beliefs and desires, and the cruder realities of a world not especially shaped to fit Johnny Magee."

John continued to borrow the teachers' books and developed the habit of reading until two and three in the morning. It was against all the rules, and he frequently burnt holes in his sheets in his efforts to make the bedclothes provide the necessary black-out, but, even when he was caught, the Powers were easy on him, being reluctant to punish a boy for doing more than the daily allotment, especially one who knew more of English literature and composition than any boy who had been at the school.

They saw well enough that they were dealing with no ordinary youth. "This boy's mind is subtle, imaginative, penetrating and expressive," wrote his English master. The woman, who came from Hartford once or twice a week to tutor him in Greek, described him as "intelligent, cooperative and capable", but noted that at times he did no more work than he absolutely had to, which echoed earlier Rugby laments. The masters all felt the charm of the six-foot boy with the humorous, twinkling eyes, just growing out of awkward adolescence, and enjoyed his ebullient mind.

The boys, on the whole, thought less of him than the teachers.

Apart from his ability to read his Virgil or Cicero in the original as though they were the morning paper, which made him precious to his fellow students in the Latin course as a kind of walking "trot", and the virility and daring which made him apparently ready for any escapade or adventure at almost any time, the fact that he gave a large part of his leisure to the setting up and printing of a little volume of his poems was not conducive to dispelling the impression in the minds of his schoolmates that he was a queer fish.

Avon, with its tradition that the training of the hand is essential to the training of the mind, had a completely equipped printing-shop, whose guiding spirit, Max Stein, had the gift of conveying to his pupils his own enthusiasm for his art. John did an admirable job with his little book, revealing taste in typography and an eye for "clean proof". His foreword was surprisingly graceful, the ability to write light-footed prose being rather rarer in a boy of seventeen than ingenuity in rhyming. He asks disarmingly that the poems be read "not too critically"—which has no doubt been the prayer of poets since the first hand struck the first lyre—"and that they be permitted by the Muses to give some pleasure to my contemporaries, but more particularly to those for whom Youth is but a laughing ghost of the Long Ago."

The volume begins with a "Sonnet after Catullus", celebrating—a bit prematurely, perhaps—

> *"a life of careless love*
> *Unharried by the vapidness of Age."*

An adult, knowing the prep-school mind, can fairly hear the shrieks of wicked delight of his schoolmates at the final line:

> *"And lip to lip we'll kiss for evermore,"*

as associated with shy, sensitive, almost feminine Johnny Magee.

A "Sonnet to Rupert Brooke" revealed a pre-occupation with the poet-turned-soldier which was to prove more than romantic hero-worship.

> *"We laid him in a cool and shadowed grove*
> *One evening, in the dreamy scent of time,*
> *Where leaves were green, and whispered high above—*
> *A grave as humble as it was sublime;*
> *There, dreaming in the fading deeps of light—*
> *The hands that thrilled to touch a woman's hair;*
> *Brown eyes, that loved the Day, and looked on Night,*
> *A soul that found at last its answered prayer . . .*
>
> *"There daylight, as a dust, slips through the trees,*
> *And drifting, gilds the fern about his grave—*

Where even now, perhaps, the evening breeze
Steals shyly past the tomb of him who gave
New sight to blinded eyes; who sometimes wept—
A short time dearly loved; and after,—slept!"

There were various attempts at jocosity, not too successful. It was the love poems—some of which have already been quoted—which gave the little book its flavor and its fragrance. Even those which gave the impression that they were written by an octogenarian looking back over a long road of disillusionment and general woe, had lines which woke shyly to life and said something about love at sixteen.

"Who can forget white lilies in the spring,
The agony of poppies, stabbing corn?
—Do you remember once when I was king,
And you my queen, how on the perfect lawn
We ruled the daisies while we laughed at play?
. . . And I must live, to see the colours start
To life; when all the world is young in May,
And honeysuckle rushes to the heart . . .

"I will not die, while roses laugh in June,
When Beauty wanders through slow, secret ways,
And sombre winter leaps again to mirth. . . .
Oh! Death comes swift and cold, and all too soon—
And I must live, while sleepy summer days,
And You—and You—are lovely on the earth!"

Critics might smite him for mating *corn* and *lawn* but it would be a dull soul that would not respond to the rush of honeysuckle to the heart.

13

The long winter term, a trial alike to pupils and faculty in any school, wore to its close. John spent a part of the Spring vacation with Nanking friends, on furlough in Connecticut. The Thomsons found the young sceptic a little ill at ease at first in the religious atmosphere of a transplanted missionary home, but, when he consented at last to relax, he was the headlong and delightful "Ian" of his Chinese boyhood, with laughing eyes and voluble tongue. He liked to sing

> *"Mad dogs and Englishmen*
> *Go out in the noonday sun,"*

and to get off a patter in cockney: "Procrystination, lydies an' gen'lemen, is the footstool to fortune. Come in your bare feet, an' go aw'y in your motor-cars." John had what is known as a "line", but when, at a local firemen's ball, he gallantly took pity on what appeared to be an unappreciated maiden, he met his Waterloo. The best he could do inspired nothing but a grunt and a plea at last that he lead her back to her husband!

Spring at Avon brought rowing in the eight-oar shell, and the black flag of revolt in a new area when John informed his father—a devoted son of Yale—that he had decided to go to Harvard. From what he had gathered, John wrote, Yale was dominated by convention. Yale boys tended to look, talk, think alike; individualism was frowned upon.

"Not that I would have it deliberately fostered in youth, but I do think that its suppression in those who believe that they have something to give thereby is little short of a social crime. And it is in seeking an atmosphere not altogether Philistine to free thought that I have decided that Harvard is, perhaps, the place for me." He was looking for real culture and intellectual stimulus, "of the kind that emanates chiefly from people in whom Philosophy, Imagination and the Comic Spirit abound," and Harvard seemed the place which had it to give.

His Harvard heresy subsided when he found that Larry Viles, who he hoped would be his roommate, was going to Cornell. Meanwhile, no promise of intellectual stimulation, in the future, or any gin rickey in skirts, in the present, seemed to diminish John's feeling that he ought to be in England. He had long got over what he called "the pacifist phase". "My conclusions," he had written his father the previous August, speculating as to what he would do in case war came, "are simply that every man alive is a pacifist at heart, but that there are times when impracticality adumbrates the question of Right or Wrong (though I realize that this is morally lax). So I should probably fight"— underscored. He was still a very young man, using very big words.

Lying on top of a tower in the sun at Avon, one Spring afternoon, John turned abruptly to his companion and announced, "Well, I think I'll join the R.A.F."

"My nostalgic tendencies, far from diminishing," he wrote his mother, "seem to be increasing with the days. Perhaps it is because I have been over here six months now, and have accomplished nothing. Not that I ever did much else, but the drive to *create* has gone, and, while I am aware of its absence, there doesn't seem to be anything I can do about it. I think the real reason is because I don't feel things so strongly. Whereas, before, there were flights through the clouds and at the same time sinkings to the lowest depths, now there is just a sort of numbness; neither one way nor the other.

"At times it worries me intensely, and I feel myself slipping from the 'awareness' (being the only word I can think of) I used to live in, but generally I am utterly unconcerned about it. I can't tell you what I'm trying to say—I must sound like some anaemic malingerer before a psychoanalyst! Have you ever had the feeling of having been able to do something once, but now have lost the art? That's how I feel."

He was obsessed, he wrote Geoffrey Sergeant, by the fear that the fire in him—"my own natural enthusiasm for things"—was being slowly smothered. "Even now, after six months in this country, I feel myself wanting to go off anywhere where there are lights, women, and noisy voices, summoning to sin of one kind or another. Everyone over here (and they are at *peace!*) seems to be fleeing in terror from Reality—anything to capture the mind for a brief moment, and so allow it to forget. The natural processes of thinking and feeling are swallowed up in an abyss of lewd entertainment. And this is the country that is supposed to be preserving and cherishing the ideals that Europe is losing! All I can say is," he concluded his jeremiad, "I think Europe is doing better, at war!

"Pardon, my dear Geoffrey, this incoherent outburst. The wireless, next door, rasps loudly of Death and Scotch alternately, and I am utterly unable to concentrate. Why is there always Noise? I wake at night and hear the same sounds ringing in my ears—endless, meaningless Noise, whereas, before, I woke to silence, and the measureless thrill of sensing eternity, to the cries of night-birds—'in hearts at peace, under an English heaven'! At times I think I am going mad with yearning—the vain and insistent groping to be back in the past, when the wind blew in my face from the Channel, and all was ecstasy! Meanwhile, England must remain a dream, and I must go on pretending to myself that I am happy here.

"I am finding it terribly difficult to express myself, Geoff! All I can say is that I am like a fish out of water, to use the old cliché—but this time it's more appropriate than ever. But what can I do about it? They won't let me back to England: the poetry is dying in me: I am in such a state of utter helplessness about it!"

England! Always England. But what he was yearning for was not a green and storied island, nor even a friendly people, revitalized by disaster, and facing appalling peril with incredible courage. He hungered for the challenge to high thinking and decent living, presented by the spirit of Thomas Arnold and the living presence of Hugh Lyon; the challenge to aspiration, beyond earthly wisdom and human daring, of Geoffrey Sergeant and the vice-master of Trinity; the challenge to integrity and discipline and constancy of his inaccessible Diana.

He had no illusions about England's being any less materialistic than his own country. In his "Brave New World" he had said his say about "the game of money, banks and houses" which he saw around him in Britain, about the

"hollow aspirations
Competing with one another in the tawdry
Glitter and speed of machines."

He knew well enough, moreover, that America had its Lyons, its Anguses, its Geoffreys, even its Dianas, if he could find them.

Two years later, anywhere in America, he would have been confronted by the ultimate challenge. But, in the winter of 1939 and '40, no one was blowing any bugles. Not the intellectuals, whose disdain of spiritual values he devoured in the weekly journals; not the great men of the headlines, playing for points while the world went up in flame; certainly not the girls, the silver-scaled and avid, who rose to any bait and all but leapt into the boat.

And John Magee was heartsick because no one in America dared him to be as magnificent as, away down deep, he wanted to be.

14

The school year wore tediously to a close and, on a memorable June 9th, his eighteenth birthday, his wise, austere yet warm-hearted father—who had been an expert tap-dancer in his youth and still preserved a hearty strain of Irish gaiety—arrived in New York from China, and his companionable, vigorous mother with the three younger boys arrived from England. It was a notable reunion. John had yearned for it, and dreaded it. They would find him changed, he had warned both his father and mother, older, not only in years, and even more independent than before. He had been on his own, he had seen the world. "I have had to take the reins of my own life in hand, whereas before you controlled them. I don't think you can expect to pick them up again just where you left off. They have passed into my hands, admittedly, at an early age, but the important thing is that they are *mine* now.

"Please don't consider this to be any kind of histrionic ultimatum. I only want you to foresee what will happen when we are together again. I foresee no little conflict on that, and other scores, and, though I hate to admit it, I look forward to our family reunion with no little trepidation!"

His apprehension failed to take into account that parents grow with their responsibilities no less than children.

John, who had enjoyed Martha's Vineyard on his brief visit the previous year, manoeuvred his family into taking a cottage near Oak Bluffs, and they spent a lively summer, with John more heartily of the family than he had ever been before. He acquired a driver's license, after one experimental turn at the wheel—"a solitary lesson was all that stood between me and the examiner," he wrote a friend, "that fateful day when a license was made out to Magee" —and promptly shook an ancient Ford V-8 to pieces on the Island's rugged roads. Her successor, a huge second-hand Packard, which they called Mephistopheles, proved more stalwart. John was a reckless driver but happily quick enough in his reactions to avoid catastrophe, and sufficiently interested in mechanics to lie under the ancient hack for hours, his long legs protruding, tinkering until the stalled mare ran again.

Observant elders watched him that summer in speculative wonder. They might not wholly approve of this young man's comings and goings, his self-assertiveness or his grouches. There was a touch of the poseur about him, with his Mayfair accent, his unkempt look and long hair, his tales of romantic deviltry which sounded authentic enough but never wholly convinced his friends. "Perhaps," wrote a boy who loved him, "you could say he was a clever showman who had something to show." But, exhibitionist, genius or pain-in-the-neck, here, beyond question, was a person who could not be ignored, a dynamo, an insatiable seeker, perpetually trying to find out what life was all about, why he was alive and what he was supposed to do about it. His speech, like his pipe, was of Oxford or Pall Mall, and his heart might be incorrigibly anglophile, but his personality was American, in its energy and its push, its receptiveness to whatever might come, its exuberant joy of life.

He was living at 3600 r.p.m. Mornings on the beach, surrounded by a bevy of girls . . . dances . . . beach parties . . . occasionally a drop too much of alcohol . . . wild drives around the bay to Vineyard Haven and Edgartown or down the long road to Chilmark . . . interspersed with family readings of "Macbeth," with John in the title role, and grave discussions with his father on the state of the world or some phase of Christian living.

When his father remonstrated with him once on turning night into day, John answered, "My generation does not expect to live long, and we want to enjoy ourselves while we may."

"I think my gallivantings must have shocked you a bit during the summer," John wrote six months later to one of his former teachers, who lived at Oak Bluffs. "But actually I think I knew in my heart what the winter held in store for me and so I turned it into one grand sort of last fling. I feel now as if I had been trying to stave off somehow the manhood I felt coming upon me all too quickly. Suddenly I realized that I *didn't want to grow up.*"

The summer retained an aura in his mind, with memories of happy chatter on the beach at East Chop, and sunny hours, with a girl on either arm, looking southward from the cliffs at Gay Head. In the autumn, he was to enter Yale with a liberal scholarship in his pocket.

But that was the summer of the fall of France, following the invasion of Denmark and Norway, of the rape of Holland and Belgium, the miracle of Dunkirk; the summer of England's deadly peril and America's feverish awakening from the long dream of her security. With bombs falling in cities he knew and loved and young men dying over the rolling green meadows of England, the England of Rupert Brooke, of Rugby, of Hugh Lyon, of Diana—whom no Morgan-le-fay had been able really to supplant—the England of his mother's people and countless others he had come to love, the England of the poets, his England, Johnny Magee could not see himself settling into any academic routine, taking part in Freshman antics and dutifully roaring *bre-ke-co-ax-co-ax-co-ax* across the football field.

The impulse to join the R.A.F. which had come upon him on the tower at Avon that spring had grown and become a determination.

His father demurred. John was only eighteen, too young to enlist. "If England goes down, it will be within the next three months. Even if you joined up immediately, you couldn't do anything about it. Enter Yale as you planned. If, in the course of the next year or two, you still feel you ought to enlist, I'll face the question with you."

That seemed to John both sound and fair and he made arrangements to get his room at New Haven.

But across the North Sea and the Channel, through a grim September, swept the black clouds of Nazi bombers. The effect on John was unmistakable.

After preoccupied days and restless nights he confronted his parents with a renewed determination. "I just can't go to college. I've never felt so deeply about anything before. I've got to get into this." Which meant, reduced to details, the Royal Canadian Air Force.

To John's father, his declaration was a return of the nightmare he had hoped he had overcome once and for all. John's mother, proud that he felt so deeply for the country of her birth, did not wholly share her husband's fears. Both recognized that their son's restlessness was no mere symptom of boyish enthusiasm, but something that came out of the deepest and best in a nature perpetually in conflict. Out of reserves of faith and courage, stored up through a lifetime of Christian living, they faced and accepted it. Surely such offering of a life as their son proposed to make came from God and was a part of His plan for them all. "Do what you feel you should do. If it is to go into the Canadian Air Force, you have our consent."

John went to see President Seymour of Yale, an old friend of his father's. John, who was nothing if not headstrong, had developed respect for the amenities. He didn't want the President to think that he failed to appreciate the opportunities Yale was offering him.

The President, who had himself been educated in England, was sympathetic. Obviously the decision, he pointed out, must be John's own. In general, he believed that young men in John's position were likely, in the end, to render greater service if they accepted the educational opportunities offered them. If, however, John's inclination against college was so strong that he would not be able to concentrate happily upon his studies, he, the President, could not urge him to enter.

"I was so taken with him and his approach to the problem," the President wrote John's father, "that I am deeply disappointed, in a personal sense, that apparently he is not to be with us, but there can be no question of the depth of his feeling. I think it is entirely likely that he would be unhappy here under present conditions. I hope that you will not feel that I let you down in not bringing the strongest sort of pressure to bear upon him, but, in all conscience, I believe that this is the kind of problem which can only be settled by the man himself."

Late in September, father and son were together in New York, preparatory to his departure for Canada. It was a Sunday evening, and John's flame of the moment, whose name was Suzanne, was dining with them. John was moved by the imminence of his departure on what he knew was, with all its glamour, a perilous adventure, a little sobered by the prospect, and reaching out for some kind of security.

"Don't think you have to stay with me," his father said. "If you want to have a good time I don't want to stand in your way."

"I want to be with you."

"What would you like to do?"

"I'd like to go to church. I want to go away in that atmosphere."

So they went together to evening service at Grace Church, in the Sunday solitude of Broadway and Ninth Street.

THE FLIER

1

"Terrible fortune has befallen me. Having gone to Ottawa and had an interview even with Air Marshal Breadner himself, I came back to Montreal and put in my application for the Air Force. I got my interview and medical right away but was found to be 16 pounds underweight. So they told me to go away and put on some weight and come back in two weeks. Since then I have been eating myself sick at every meal, drinking milk, stout, etc., ad infin., given up smoking and all forms of exercise and sleeping 10 or 11 hours at night. Have gained half a pound. I only have to gain 4 to 6 pounds for them to accept me. (They will overlook 10 pounds underweight, but not 16 pounds.) What on earth am I going to do? I've simply *got* to get in, I'll die of chagrin if I don't. If determination will get me in, I'm in. . . . I can't tell you how miserable I am. Give me some hints about getting *fat!*"

That is John Magee to the life—intensity, desperation and all—writing his mother from Canada, in October, 1940. Somehow, he gains not six pounds but fifteen and is actually overweight when the doctor gives him his "medical".

It is in that fashion that John Magee becomes A/C2—aircraftsman, second grade—Royal Canadian Air Force. "Life is wonderful!" he writes exultantly.

Getting his inoculations and gathering together his equipment in the over-crowded, gray stone Manning Depot at

Toronto, he catches intimations of an Air Force apparently congested and disorganized.

"I took my first inoculation rather badly and have felt like the devil since yesterday," he writes home. "Still the thought of escaping confinement tomorrow, and being at liberty to look at my militarized and be-uniformed reflection in shop windows! I sleep in a large hall with about 1500 other men in two-layer berths, but they are not too bad, really. The food is not designed for the most sensitive palates, as you can imagine, but that is just one of the *Ardua* to be undergone before the *Astra* come in sight."

The reference is to the motto of the Canadian Royal Air Force, which reminds romanticists that there are bumps on the way to the stars.

From the Depot he is sent to Trenton, Ontario, for "security guard", pending a vacancy at an Initial Training School, "a deadly business", he writes his brother, "involving sentry duty for a period 'not exceeding two weeks'. Well, the class before us was here eight weeks, and we shall be lucky if we are in Initial (Ground) Training School, our next step, by Christmas . . ." "We go on duty every other day and night in 4-hour shifts, 4 on, 4 off, and if you think it's easy," he writes a friend, "let buffoon's ears grow from the side of your skull . . . It is about 5 above zero on a cold night. Our 'free' day is taken up with lectures on gas, armaments, flying, etc. The food is rather poor, really. We get nothing that can't be cooked in buckets—endless potatoes (mashed—beaten to pulp), mashed turnips, mashed beets (canned), but never any green vegetables, and never any fresh fruit. And the resulting super-abundance of starch is ruining our complexions, which, in turn, ruins our glamour, which in turn, ruins our popularity with the opposite sex (when and if we see 'em)." "I might add that Trenton is a training school for cooks!!! Still," he continues, "it seems rather fatuous to be discontented with life while it lasts."

He already has three cronies, an Englishman from the Bahamas, a Scotsman, who has lived most of his life in Canada, and a Yorkshireman, called Barney, "with a terrific accent. He is a scream. He has been in Rumania, Venezuela, and practically everywhere in the oil business. He hopes to be an observer. The other two and self, of course, hope to become fighter pilots." His chances are not too good. Practically "every man here wants with all his heart to be a pilot; one out of ten will. The only thing we can be sure of is England by the summer. I can hardly believe it! I only wish I had joined up long ago so that I should be there now."

The days are filled with hard work, the long Canadian nights are lonely. "Letters mean more to me than ever up here. When anyone gets a letter he is forced to read the universally accepted paragraphs aloud, by a long-standing, though self-created, tradition, whereby the loneliest heart among us may derive a sort of vicarious comfort from another's homely news!"

Guard duty is a bore when you want with all your heart and soul to get into the air, into training and through with it, and on to England, where the battle is—and the glory.

John is thinking a good deal about glory and *dulce et decorum est*. The notion that it is both sweet and seemly to die for your country is sentimental tosh, of course, he tells himself, but . . . He likes to philosophize about it all, the Past, the Present, the Future (with capitals) and "Alfred Lord Tennyson's" idea (probably mistaken) that "I am a part of all that I have met." His boyish mind is a jumble of youthful cynicism and sentimentalism, of a girl he has fallen in love with, and thinks he would like to marry, a Czechoslovakian pianist in Toronto, of quotations from Racine and Baudelaire, of spiritual aspiration and thoughts of a life hereafter, and of his own possible obituary. Suppose he should be killed? Will people get sugary about "this bright young star gone out from the heavens," this "vivid voice silenced in its very prime," and make a starry-eyed poet-warrior of him? "Perhaps," he writes his brother, "that is why I want to die, in circumstances violently heroic, so that they'll never know . . ." So that, in other words, they will do exactly what he deplores. "And a cement epitaph," he writes another correspondent—for when he has an idea that he likes, he lets all his friends have it in almost the same words—"a cement epitaph would blind them to the fact that I would never have been anything but an impoverished cynic." It might not be bad at that. "I have a sort of morbid curiosity about death."

He flies on leave to Toronto and, returning after the designated deadline, is caught "by a sergeant who dislikes me," John writes a friend, "because I call him Mei-Mei." That was Chinese for "little sister". "Am now in jail." A Catholic priest calls on him and asks him what is wrong with his life.

"Tubercular Jamaicans are said to crawl strangely underground at dead of night," is John's cryptic reply.

"Father O'Keefe failed to see the humor of it," he reports, "and I got an extra two days in the klink for disrespect in addressing the chaplain."

He is still a boy—barely half past eighteen—torn between the sternness of life and the absurdity of the idea that it could possibly be stern for him. On sentry guard, before five in the morning, writing,—against the rules—writing with gloves on, in the bitter cold, he gives his father and mother a sublimated expression of his struggle between reality and literariness.

"I'm in a sand-bagged machine-gun post, with a Lewis gun in front of me. From my vantage point I could rake the whole aerodrome, if need be. This is indeed a symbolic and powerful position." He does not elucidate the symbolism, and leaves obscure in what sense his position is "powerful", except that he might, if he went crazy, do considerable damage. "Above me the stars, in all their brittle intensity,"—Can any budding writer miss that word *brittle?* —"The stars . . . seem to watch with me through the long night's vigil, and I am not alone. With all its discomforts, this is the life! The throb of an aeroplane engine is music in my ears now. It has all the power of Beethoven, the grandeur of Wagner, and the eagerness and intensity of Strauss. . . .

"I have become one of a group of men, who are all, to the last man, resigned to death and even anxious for it— or, if not for death, at least for the chance of showing their mettle. Talk of the war is *verboten* among us. We speak only of the past and the present. The future for us does not exist. We compare notes on shows, books, women, and all the lovely, trivial things of life. It is no good trying to talk reason to any of us. We are living deliberately in a sort of grand, illusory, but terribly precious, fool's paradise." . . . "The whole place," he writes a friend, "thrills to the vivid, eager living of men who realize that they are almost certainly in their last year of life." . . .

"An aeroplane is to us not a weapon of war, but a flash of silver slanting the skies; the hum of a deep-voiced motor; a feeling of dizziness; it is speed and ecstasy. And, so you see, we pass our days. At Trenton we are absolutely out of touch with the world. A newspaper is tacitly taboo and we never know the time of day, let alone the date. In short, it is a world by itself. And now, good my mother, I bid you a cold good night."

It is altogether a boy speaking, with the solemnity and the selfconsciousness of youth and a side-glance at the literary graces.

2

It is a far cry from an ice-bound Canadian training field to a cottage on the North Devon coast, but the memory of an Easter vacation of exaltation and high resolve returns, and John sits down to write a letter he has for months had on his mind. He has not written Geoffrey Sergeant since his induction in the Air Force. What will Geoffrey say of his abandonment of the ideal of non-violence of which they had caught so bright a glimpse in the relative calm of the Easter of 1939?

"It has been difficult to write you since I took this rather final step. I know, Geoff, how sorry you will be that everything has not worked out for me in the way that we had hoped. But I think that convictions, however zigzag and contradictory a course they run, should be followed at any price. Hence my presence here. I decided that the things of democracy are worth fighting for, though I feel no antipathy to the Germans. And that's that. . . . Apologies, dear Geoff, for a fallen ideal, but I hope it will not come between us."

Geoffrey, in South Africa, working as an operating theatre assistant in a military hospital, instructing in First Aid and ambulance duties, recognizes that only "the highest of motives" have impelled John to join the military forces, and, instead of resenting his apostasy, loves him the more for the magnanimity which will not let him spurn the friend of other days and other dreams.

Meanwhile, not even the highest motives can sustain themselves in John perpetually on the top level.

"We are getting frightfully sick of our job," he writes home. "Snow has been falling for about two weeks or more now. Not gentle, friendly Christmas-card snow, but driving particles of icy matter that burn into the skin and clutch at the very soul with freezing fingers."

His father and mother and three brothers have gone to live in Washington, and make him homesick with their accounts of the comfortable three-story house on Bancroft Place, just off Connecticut Avenue, which he scarcely dares call "ours", since he himself may never see it. "Suddenly I am feeling very tired of all the old virtues—nobility, patriotism, manliness, and courage. The old familiar faces of the past seem so much more significant. But, in my heart of hearts, I am glad to be suffering for the country I love so well—more than ever, now that I shall be seeing it in a few months. Still the old lie, '*dulce et decorum est*', runs ironically through my mind, reminding me of the high ideals with which soldiers are supposed to be enthused; whereas, in reality, serving one's country is not a glamorous crusade, nor any golden fleece, but rather best described simply as 'inevitable duty'. But we are going through the toughest period now. I find it needs plenty of 'guts' to stick to a rifle in the nocturnal snow when there are beds and warmth within. But it is good training for us and every one of us realizes that these little trials will help prepare us for the greater ones overseas."

Life is strenuous in Trenton. Up at dawn and late to bed. Never more than five hours' sleep. When, months after the ordeal is over, he returns for a visit and the Commanding

Officer of the Security Guard asks archly, "Really, Mr. Magee, don't you feel that, all in all, you had a pretty good time here?" John gives him a look which he describes in a letter home as "of such ferocity that he turned and practically trotted away with his tail between his legs."

No, Trenton is tough. No one had forewarned him of this particular ordeal. Oh, to get to the Elementary Training School! There is a bottle-neck somewhere. But it is something even to examine passes at the aerodrome gate "under the magnificent and sort of baronial"—one wonders why "baronial" except that the word rumbles and resounds—"baronial tutelage of the Aurora Borealis". And he is feeling ridiculously healthy, "after being the walking shadow that I was this summer. I should be putting on a great deal more weight, if I only could get more sleep." He catches German measles and recovers.

"In the pink, working at tremendous pressure . . . Doing very moderately in Link trainer . . . a toy plane mounted on a control-box. Actually it is harder to fly than a real plane, the controls being far more sensitive. It responds to any movement of the throttle, joy-stick and rudder-bar as does a real plane, and is an invaluable aid in training for the fast fighter-ships of today."

"Am now 'Aircraftsman—first class' and, when I graduate from here (if), will be L/A/C (leading aircraftsman). Then a long wait before becoming either Sergeant-Pilot or Pilot Officer. But that's in the very distant future. Thank you very much for Biblical book. My religious views shifting again, but have not crystallized."

Heaven opens momentarily with rumors of Florida or California for training, and shuts with a bang in his face.

But, even though he has not yet begun his actual training in the air, flying anywhere is beginning to seem better to him than doing anything else in any other place in the world. "What was once simply a flying noisiness," he writes a friend, "an incomprehensible machine, has become . . . a live and poised animal that breathes; it is a dizziness, an eager and sensitive thing; it is power; it is speed, and ecstasy. In fact, my dear old friend, the worst has happened, and I wish you to forget and cast me off; for I have become *airminded!!*"

Christmas brings a quick trip home. The family circle is impressed, first, by the uniform and then by what is inside it. "What," asks brother David, aged fifteen, and Christopher, twelve, "what has happened to John?"

In St. John's Church on Lafayette Square, opposite the White House, Sunday morning, John whispers to his mother during the service that he would like to stay for Holy Communion. He has been "off church" for two years, and his father, assistant rector of St. John's, can hardly go through the ritual of the Sacrament, so moved he is, as he gives his son the bread and the wine.

3

Early in the new year, John is at the Elementary Flying School at St. Catherine's, Ontario, "the toughest station in the whole of Canada," and is making his solo-flight after six hours in the air, when the average is between ten and eleven. "My instructor is most encouraging. Said I was the most exceptional pupil he had ever had, and he thought I would be a valuable man in the service, etc. Result— J. G. M. cheers up a bit."

Whereupon he proceeds to do his best to terminate his promising career.

"Do you know what a spin is?" he writes his parents. "It is a horrid, sickening spiral dive towards the ground (*ghastly* and terrifying sensation). Well, I asked my instructor if we could do one. He demurred, but I really wanted to, so we did. Soon I learned—or thought I learned —to do one myself (you can do one purposely to practise getting out of it) and he was very pleased, but warned me never to do one alone. That was yesterday.

"Last night I realized they had a sort of morbid attraction for me—possibly because they were so terrifying (N.B. the engine is off and all you hear is the wind screaming in the flying wires). Today I was told to go to 3,000 feet and practise steep turns. On the way up, a little devil kept telling me that I could easily do a spin if I got out of sight of the aerodrome, and nobody would be any the wiser. But it also taunted me for being *afraid!* I fought the thing during the long climb skywards, and finally, in a fit of impatience, decided to do one.

"So, instead of levelling off as instructed, I continued climbing for 20 minutes until I was at the tremendous height of 6,500 feet, when I thought it safe to try, and let her go. As soon as I was in it I realized something was wrong. I had the feel of being slightly *upside down* yet still spinning. The ground was whirling before me when suddenly my safety belt snapped, and in the same moment I realized I was in an *inverted* spin, something I have only read of in heavy black type in flying manuals. My head hit the cockpit cowling and I came out of the seat. All the time I was hurtling like a corkscrew towards the earth. I had no idea how to get out of the thing. I applied full opposite rudder, but it made me spin all the faster.

"By this time my eyes were bulging out of my head and my ears blocked. I heaved on the control (joystick) column frantically but couldn't move it as I could not pull very hard with my safety belt bust. I think I became unconscious then. The next thing I remember is making one last effort and feeling myself pressed back into my seat as the nose came up. I remember my altimeter needle trembling between 700 and 800 feet. I had dropped almost 5000 *feet* in about 20 seconds! As the ship levelled out, I relapsed into a state of semi-fogginess, and, when I regained full use of my senses, I headed straight for home but had to circle the field twice before plucking up the guts to land.

"My instructor came running out and started to give me a good going over (he had watched the whole thing) but I was too dazed to listen. But he climbed into the rear cockpit and took me straight up again and immediately put me into two consecutive spins, later explaining that, if he hadn't, I probably would never have been able to fly again. When I finally staggered out of the plane, he put an arm around my shoulders and said: 'Laddie, you've got what it takes.' I am simply dreading that it will get to the ears of the C.O., as it would be certain to wash me out."

On the eve of his "20-hour check"—his examination after twenty hours of flying time—the physical man unexpectedly raises a protest. "I flew in clouds with my cockpit hatch open," he writes a friend, "inhaling the airy dampness with no apparent ill effects until that evening when I retired to bed with a temperature of 103°. It stayed up in astral figures while I lay delirious, babbling of things aeronautical to a bored orderly, until today, when it is normal again. I have been in bed a week, which is all very aggravating, as I have lost valuable flying time and, what is worse, missed a great many ground school lectures, in each of which a large area is covered to do with guns and other paraphernalia for which I have no mental aptitude. In fact I may miss my class through this brief illness and have to wait a month or so for the next, which will be trying."

He recovers and is grounded by the weather. On the eve of his 20-hour check, he gives up a chance to see "Gone with the Wind" to get a good night's sleep. "So much hangs in the balance. The thought of it is rather frightening. However, to counteract the fears, is its most effective enemy, annoyance, because I am so far behind now, having once been ahead of everybody. Had I not been in the hospital, I should now be worrying about my 50-hour check, instead of the 20. But such is luck!"

He comes through his test, and, having passed through the stages of Aircraftsman, second class, and Aircraftsman, first class, is L.A.C. John Magee, meaning that he is a Leading Aircraftsman.

4

He is filled with pride but not so swollen as to forget that, under the flier, is the poet. He is setting himself up, he writes his friend, Max Stein, "as a sort of 'barrackroom poet' ", and feels in need of producing the evidence. Will his friend please send him two copies of the book of verses which he had helped him print, one with which to establish himself at "St. Kitts", the other for his newest love. Tanya, the blonde, blue-eyed Czechoslovakian is now the focus of his dreams, and must learn what he can do in the way of adoration when he really tries.

He has, in fact, already given her some evidence, all her own:

THE PRAYER

Be gentle to her, grey-haired Time,
*   Walk with slow pace;*
Beat not with bitter blows
*   Against her face.*

Be generous to her, O Life,
*   Fill her with laughter,*
That there be no sad memories
*   When Death comes after.*

And thou, sad Death, be chivalrous to her,
*   Come without pain;*

Fall on her tender, smiling brow
Like summer rain.

Meanwhile, at St. Catherine's he has competition even in the field of poetry.

"This morning the squadron bugler was sick and the grimmest Flight Sergeant-major on the station burst into the barracks, raging as to why we were not up. Suddenly he stopped and said:

'Night's candles are burned out, and jocund day
Stands tiptoe on the misty mountain tops . . .
Awake! for Morning in the bowl of Night
Hath flung the stone that put the stars to flight!' "

Was ever a sergeant so beguiling or the poet of cushioned ease so inconsiderate?

On the blackboard at headquarters a round hand chalks up the daily schedule, and, one morning, John finds that he has taken a step forward in his training. Aerobatics, in and out of the fleecy fog over Ottawa, makes demands on the body and nervous system, he discovers, to which they are not accustomed. But he finds that he is bearing up under the strain. "I can now loop the loop, do a slow roll, a half roll and loop out, a stalled turn, a chandelle, and an Immelman (the hardest manoeuvre there is in a low-powered ship—you go into a loop, and when on your back at the top you roll out of it). If you aren't careful to have *exactly* the right speed you are liable to stall on your back and fall off into an inverted spin. These Immelmans are not actually on our course but they are a good thing to know in a tight corner. I have only done them with my instructor; have not yet plucked up the guts to do one alone.

"Aerobatics are very funny. You are apt to get a bit light-headed and it is a good thing to keep talking to yourself to keep 'on the ball'—but they're marvellous, as you can imagine, for the thrill they give! Flying upside down is queer," he adds, and the word seems distinctly British in its understatement. "You hang in your safety belt, and it's very hard to keep your hands and feet on the controls. They tend to fall off if you aren't careful. The rest of my 20 hours can be taken up in aerobatics and cross-country flights to other aerodromes. Out of that will come about 5 hours instrument flying. I had 40 minutes of this today—extraordinary sensation. We sit in the back cockpit, instead of the usual front, with a hood over our heads. Then you have to tell by your instruments exactly what is happening, how to correct it, etc."

Hungering as he is to become a fighter pilot, there are awful moments when he fears he is about to be sent to a flying school for training bombers. "The idea of long bombing trips over Germany by night has its appeal, but I personally would much rather revel in the speed and independence of a fighter. You see they classify us as being either 'single-engine' pilots, or 'twin-engine' pilots. After that, you stick to whichever you are chosen for."

But worse than anything is the fear of being "washed out", dropped, sent home. It has happened to others; it may happen to him; and is the stuff of which nightmares are made. But, early in March, he passes his 50-hour test and final Ground School examinations. "The assistant supervising officer here told me to do a snap half-roll and to loop out at 2000 feet. Evidently wanted to see if I would do it (aerobatics are generally done at 6000 feet). Tremendous thrill."

"Our Elementary Course is over," he writes shortly after. "Quite a few who came here with us are 'Gone with the Wind' (that is, washed out) and the remainder, having gotten this far, should complete the course successfully and find Wings—and Action—at the other end of the road.

"We have got through in record time, and the instructors seem to think we are quite an exceptional crowd. Accordingly, instead of going on leave we are going to stay on here and take a course in Formation Flying, and Advanced Aerobatics, and will be practising actual combat amongst ourselves, probably with camera guns. We shall also be having Advanced Navigation in Ground School, Signals, Radio Direction Finding, etc. It promises to be great fun. We are being 'guinea-pigged' and everyone is waiting to see what is going to happen. Normally we would be going to Service School, after some leave, but we are going to stay on here another month and put in another fifty hours' flying, so that we will have a hundred when we go to Service School. It will probably be a great advantage to have taken this experimental course, though in Primary Training Machines, so that when we join Service Squadrons we will actually have some formation experience. Of course we are in a way disappointed to have to forego our leave, but the time will come."

"Formation flying is very hard," he writes a few days later, "but a great deal of fun. The slightest jerk on the stick is enough to throw you into the next plane, which is only a few feet away. We had great fun in formation practice today. The instructors we were with happened to know of some army manoeuvres going on at Niagara-on-the-Lake (at the mouth of the river) and we came down on them suddenly through the clouds, scattering all the troops and causing tremendous havoc. Actually of course it was good practice for them, as, when we dove the second time, they had A.A. (anti-aircraft) guns out and if we had been enemy planes they could have shot us to pieces! Next time we are going to take little paper bags of flour and really go after them.

"Flew up to Lake Huron the other day, a six-hour flight. Came back very tired and stiff. Today another chap and self flew to Buffalo and had a look at Bell Aircraft, Inc. There were some Aerocobras on the ground, and, though we tried to entice them up, they wouldn't play. (We kept over the center of the river so as not actually to violate the border rules.)

"The field here is getting muddier and muddier. We have started flying at 6:30 (5:30 your time) when it's still practically dark, so as to take advantage of the frost, which hardens the ground overnight. Three planes turned over in the mud today (it's very hard to land in a 'sticky' field) and six propellers were broken by flying clods, etc. Flying is now washed out for the afternoon and at the moment we are in Ground School, pretending to improve our knowledge of the local terrain."

They live close to the edge of things, a handbreadth from the precipice, a grass-blade's width from the scythe.

"Yesterday a chap called M—who had of late rather a high opinion of himself as a flier—landed upside down on a fence at the far end of the landing field. Plane caught fire but we got him out. Apart from burns, most noticeable result in M; MODESTY! Last weekend a Harvard (our next type, if we go to Fighter School) flew over the aerodrome at low altitude in a blinding snowstorm. We couldn't see him and he couldn't see the ground. We sent up Very Lights to bring him in, which fortunately he saw, and somehow realized that he was over an aerodrome; came in and landed, heaven knows how. Much excitement, inspection of Harvard, etc. He had twenty minutes' gas left and was headed direct for Lake Ontario. If he hadn't seen our lights he would have run out of gas halfway out—very lucky."

5

The end of March, on an hour-and-a-half's notice, John's course ends and he is on his way to Toronto to await the call to Service Training Squadrons. He is ordered to the Service Flying School at Uplands, Ottawa, where all his dreams seem to come true at once. This is flying that *is* flying!

"You have no idea how fast, noisy, and generally terrifying these Harvards are. What thrills me is that planes of this type were actually used by the French against the Germans at Dunkirk. They have between eighty and ninety instruments as well as bomb-racks and machine guns (2), though we usually carry camera guns for training purposes. I have not actually soloed in one yet, although I was ready to, a week ago—the weather has always interfered. However, I have flown about ten hours solo on the Yale, an intermediate trainer rather like the Harvard, but without a retractable undercart and with a 350 instead of 600 horsepower engine."

At Uplands, flying, poetry, natural beauty, and the hard duty of learning to slaughter your fellowman in single combat come together in one breath-taking synthesis. There is a vast landing-field with hundreds of planes like enormous beetles, the rush of the yellow-bodied bees overhead, singly or in swarms, the thrill of feeling the craft rise from the earth into the blue Canadian sky, the clouds rushing past, the inland sea, blue and sparkling, far below, or the dark

forests, dotted with lakes; the faces of his mates in training, clear and resolved, with daring eyes, the officers in their
brown tunics, firm but always friendly, never forgetting that
these are free men they are training, who will not be driven,
but must understand before they can act.

"Yesterday I flew my instructor up into the Gatineau
Hills, north of Ottawa," John writes his father and mother,
"about a hundred miles 'into the interior', as non-Canadians
love to say, to a large lake with rocks and islands sticking
up all over its surface, every inch of ground covered with
bare trees; just about the most desolate spot I have ever
seen. There he took over the controls and for forty-five
minutes gave me the most thrilling low flying exhibition I
have ever dreamed of. Low-flying in a Fleet was a thrill, but
going 180 to 200, in a Harvard, six inches off the ground (or
water in this case) is really something. You haven't lived
yet, poor, earthbound mortals!

"He flew between two rocks about ten feet apart (wing
span of a Harvard is forty-two feet) like this:

and did three slow rolls in succession not more than eighty
feet off the surface of the water (the best of fliers expect
to lose a hundred feet in a roll). Just to the side of the
lake was a big rocky mountain which we climbed in cir-
cles; then down went the nose and we flew vertically down

a five-hundred-foot precipice, levelling off once more just over the water. On the way back we ran into a thunderstorm and I came the nearest to being air-sick I have yet in my aeronautical career!"

He glories in such aerial antics.

"I had some fun today. After sitting around in the flight room all afternoon I at last got hold of a boat and started out north to have a look at the mountains in the Gatineau district. After about a quarter of an hour I noticed to my surprise that someone was on my tail. Remembering the elementary lesson, I at once went into my Immelman and rolled down out of the loop so as to be on his tail; but he was nowhere to be seen. Then I looked behind me and found him still behind and above me. Realizing that this was no amateur, I throttled back until he was alongside me—and it turned out to be a brand new Grumman Gulf-Hawk, belonging to a fighter squadron at Rockcliffe, Ottawa. I had never seen one before.

"Soon we were at it again and must have manoeuvred for three-quarters of an hour, at least, he of course getting the better of me most of the time. One thing that amazed me was that, although he had twice my speed, he could still *turn inside me*, which speaks well for the ship's manoeuvrability, as generally the faster a plane the larger its turning circuit. And a Harvard is by no means clumsy. From my meager acquaintance with the Gulf-Hawk I prophesy a great future for it. It's just about the most vicious little clipper you ever saw—rather like an overgrown beetle-bug in a perpetual temper."

"I have found my place in the sun!" John writes exultantly to a former teacher, his "dear philosopher and

friend", Warner Gookin, in Martha's Vineyard. "I am finding that flying has really been in my blood all the time,
and I didn't know it! There have, of course, been endless
or seemingly endless, preliminaries, such as a long term of
apprenticeship, standing guard over an aerodrome, then a
month in Ground School, and other unpleasant details, but
it has all been worth it. . . .

"I am rather afraid that I shall emerge from this war as
a hopeless illiterate, but it seems so unimportant now. I
have almost forgotten the significance and identity of Self
in the great war machine of which I am an infinitesimal
cog. It's rather fun. Not like Germany, I imagine, where
the fact of your own unimportance is rubbed into you every
day. Here we are continually being *told* of the importance
of the individual, how it all depends on us, etc., but you
come to realize, in a far gentler way, your own insignifi-
cance, which is good for one, like myself, who has rather a
large estimation of his own importance!

"It leaves us all with the gripping—and ironical—fear
that the holocaust might have blown over before we have
our chance in the skies over England. We each have a defi-
nite urge to leave our own impress on the firmament, if
only as a black smudge while spinning to earth for the last
time. That is how distorted our perspective is becoming!"

6

Yes, John Magee has found his place in the sun, and his relation to the cosmos. Six months have made a difference. His letters tell the story, not only in what they say but in what comes up between the lines, letters dramatically different from the immature literary exercises of a half year before. Then he had been a boy, interested mainly in himself, his thoughts and his emotions, craving excitement and pleasure in the present, a glorious death and apotheosis in the future, self-centered and bookish to his fingertips. Now he is a man, objective and outgoing, interested, above all, in his job and in doing it as well as he could learn to do it. The literary phrasing, the literary references, disappear from his letters. He has eaten strong meat and lost relish for cream puffs.

Every day has its magic and its satisfaction of what has become his deepest inner craving. But life is not all aerobatics and thrills. And one day a Jinx takes the seat beside him, and everything begins to go wrong. With his Wings just over the next cloud!

"This has been an unpleasantly eventful week for me so far," he writes his father and mother. "On Saturday I got lost and made a forced landing up in the Gatineau Mountains near a tiny village called Notre Dame de la Salette, where there wasn't even a telephone. It took me about three hours to hitch-hike back to Ottawa where I was severely reprimanded (a) for getting lost, (b) for misjudging my petrol supply so as to have had to make a forced landing and (c) for taking so long to get back. None of these eventualities were exactly preventable and I felt rather unjustly treated. I suppose I might have watched my bearings rather more closely but at best I am no ace navigator."

That was bad enough, but worse was to come. He was ordered to report for night flying at three the next morning and set and tested his alarm-clock to go off at 2:30 A.M.

"I woke up at 4:10 and of course it was too late to do anything about it, so I went back to sleep again, trying to think of some explanation for the morrow. When I went over to fly in the morning I found I was 'on charge' for missing N-F. This is a significant affair in the Air Force. It's a sort of minor version of a court-martial, and if you once get on charge it goes on your records and automatically disqualifies you from getting a commission. I have only been on charge once before, which was at Trenton, for not shining my buttons on parade! That, however, was struck off my record after six months. But now at this final stage I have another charge on record and I am thoroughly disgusted."

He wanted a commission "more than anything in the world" but, even with a spotless record, commissions were getting harder and harder to achieve. He had been gradually resigning himself to going overseas as a sergeant pilot and having to salute all his school friends, but the hope for a commission had remained. Now to have it thus blighted! There was wormwood in the discovery that he was "top dog" in his class for a commission.

"All of no avail now. You can't imagine how miserable I feel about the whole thing. It seems so *petty* that something, so easy to go wrong on, should decide one's future to such an extent, but I suppose they must draw the line somewhere."

And the Jinx wasn't through with him yet. It had, in fact, hardly got into action.

"I am in the dog house," he wailed to his friend Guy Stoker, in Montreal. "I crossed swords with a pilot officer in our flight several weeks ago, and, having got his knife into me, he is screwing it around in my back. He framed (actually, *framed!*) me on a charge a fortnight ago for which I lost half my prospects of a commission (which were, as I later discovered, the best in my class until that point, *mirabile dictu*). Today, however, a climax occurred when he followed, in a surreptitious manner, another chap and self, doing formation flying. After about 45 miles we broke it up for a breather and had a little dogfight. In came the P/O, whom neither of us recognized. So we ganged up on him and had a wonderful time.

"Suddenly I recognized him and immediately disengaged, and left in a long diving turn for home, hoping he had not got my number. After a couple of minutes I looked around, and, sighting a following aircraft, slowed down to 180 (from 275) and let him catch up, thinking I'd made a pretty damn good getaway and this was my No. 2 coming back into formation. Needless to say it was the P/O, who got my number, did a couple of sarcastic pylon turns around me and left.

"Now we are both on charge for:
  (1) Taking off in formation (which we didn't do, though we were quite close)
  (2) Not flying formation all the time
  (3) Doing something else instead

(4) To wit, unauthorized aerial combat
(5) Driving an aircraft over 262 m.p.h.
(6) Low flying at 700 feet, to which altitude he forced
    me down on disengaging.

"God knows what will come of it all. One can only forecast with safety that I shall be barred from getting a commission and I may very well be grounded for a month and set back a course or alternately washed out altogether. But I have got to the point where I don't really give a damn anyway. I foresee weeks of C.B."—confined to barracks—"ahead, which will be good, as I may get some studying done. After which we will dine together and I shall weep profusely as I tell you my troubles. . . .

"Seriously, old man, I am most discouraged. I have tried like mad to keep my nose clean in this place, but it hasn't worked. My only consolation is that I am a cinch for the fighter command, which is my greatest desire! Heigh-ho!"

"I am getting a court-martial some time this week," he writes another friend, Robert Mitchell, "and may be washed out, failed, or set back a couple of courses, the prospects of all of which are not very pleasing. I don't think they'll wash me out as I have pretty good flying marks but it seems so damn senseless to contemplate retarding my career when England is crying for fliers. This is just an instance of the workings of that infernal machine, the Military Mind."

He misjudged that mind or it functioned, for once, contrary to its own nature, for John speaks no more in his letters of a court-martial. Possibly the M.M. was not as senseless in the emergency as L/A/C Magee feared.

But, even though the court-martial fails to materialize, the Jinx has other items in her bag of tricks.

"Interesting occurrence today," John goes on in his letter to Guy Stoker. "Drained the last drop of gas out of my crate 500 feet from the runway. Motor stopped, and I came in with no engine between a T.C.A. boat and the control car, missing former by 6″ and latter by –1″. In other words, I brushed the top of it with my wheels.

"Which reminds me that, since we last met, I had a lovely crack-up. I stalled too high off the ground at night and spun in from about 30 feet, did a lovely cartwheel, completely demolishing an aircraft. One wing was torn off, the other rumpled up like a concertina. The propeller shattered.

"I wasn't even scratched. I think I'd have been happier if I had been but I felt supremely ridiculous sitting in a twisted fuselage without a scratch! and the undercarriage was wiped out. For all of which I lost my good name as a flier. And so it is, Guy, that my career has been by no means distinguished to date."

To his parents he writes the sad details.

"Monday night I did something which affected my reputation as a flier, which has been unbelievably good to date, and was my one consolation. I misjudged a night landing and crashed on the runway, totally destroying a $35,000 aircraft but not even scratching myself. I was thrown clear (luckily my safety belt broke off) on the grass just off the runway. I don't think I have ever been so utterly mortified in my life. If I had been hurt myself I might have felt better about it! Then again it wouldn't have been so bad (a) if it hadn't been my fault and (b) if I hadn't been in the 'doghouse' already. But, coming on top of all that, it sort of shattered me.

"It was early morning before I had pulled myself together enough to fill out all the accident reports and written a letter to the C.O., describing the accident (a local formality), and it was a very tired, angry, and thoroughly disgusted John Magee who crawled into bed just as the bugle was blowing in the morning. I was grounded all yesterday and spent the rest of the day going from brass-hat to brass-hat and getting all the callings down you can imagine. I barely escaped getting on charge again for my negligence in misjudging the flare-path.

"Since it's all over now, I might as well describe what happened. I came in out of the circuit, having been flying one and a half hours and feeling about ready for bed. Everything seemed all right until I was approaching the end of the flare-path. Suddenly I began to feel that something was wrong. I glanced at my air-speed indicator which read 85 m.p.h. Rather low, I thought (the Harvard's landing speed is 90 to 95 m.p.h.), and put my nose down a bit to gain the extra speed necessary. Then I couldn't figure out just how high I was. One's idea of elevation is not very good at night. A light looks the same at a hundred feet as it does at ten— at least as far as I can make out.

"Suddenly, I found out that I was practically on the ground and my immediate reaction was to pull the nose up. If I had remembered to hit the throttle I would have been O.K. but in the thrill of the moment I forgot it. The aircraft started up again and stalled about twenty feet off the ground. Immediately I lost control. A wing dropped and I dropped onto a wing-tip. There was a terrific jar, then I was thrown out of my seat as the plane cartwheeled around the wing-tip and dug her nose in, I landing on my face feeling very silly and angry.

"The plane looked so funny, sort of grovelling around, that I was almost tempted to laugh. Then all was still and I sat and swore silently for about a minute until a car came dashing out with the fire truck and ambulance behind it. It contained my own instructor, who happened to be Flying Control Officer for that night.

"He didn't know who it was and when I told him, 'Yes, it's Magee,' he gave a little laugh and said, 'I might have known. You've certainly been having yourself a field day, haven't you?'

"Anyway, he was so nice about it that I crawled into the back of the car and cried like a baby. I ought, I suppose, to be grateful for avoiding any black eyes, but I can't help feeling rather mortified that what started out to be such a promising career had to go and spoil itself like that. I think I was very lucky not to be washed out. At least I am still going to get my Wings."

The punishments sternly meted out by the "brass-hats" were, in fact, exceptionally mild. A restriction of privileges, no canteen, no late passes, and pack drill every day. And eleven days, washing planes at the rate of two hours a day.

"It's a great life! I thought of applying for a week's leave to get rested up but I don't want to impress them too much with the fact that I can't take it! I am passed fit for flying duties now, and am up again for night flying tonight. I should be frightened except for the fact that I've had so much bad luck that the law of averages, if nothing else, demands that I get a good break once in a while! Meanwhile, *Excelsior*—Onward and Upward!"

The final examinations proved, among other things, that his Jinx had removed himself.

"Knowing me to be the mechanized moron I am"— meaning, rather, one assumes, "moron at mechanics"—"I am sure that you will readily agree, with all my Ground School instructors, that Providence must have had a hand. All the results are not out yet, but I got 197/200 in Navigation, and 91/100 in Armament. I came first in Navigation and second in Armament. The other results are not out yet. In my Flying I had a mixture of success and comparative failure. In my Instrument Test (blind flying) I started off on the wrong foot and never got right again. My take-off (blind) was all right until I tried to pull the undercart up, but it stuck. While endeavoring to get it working, I omitted to uncage my directional gyro, which registered oo degrees ahead when all the time I was turning! That rather shook me up and I stank all the way through.

"That afternoon it became very hazy. You couldn't see the sun. My only consolation, as I sat in Ground School in the afternoon, was that I wasn't having my Wings Test that day, when all of a sudden a corporal came in and said Magee was wanted for his Wings Test.

"My heart fell to my boots, because everyone who flies knows that he can fly well one day and not the next. I was panic-stricken, as I knew it was an 'off day' for me—and it was so hazy you couldn't see the ground from a thousand feet. And there was no horizon. However, I reported at the Flight Room and found, to add to my despair, that I had drawn the toughest marker on the station. It was a very nervous I who climbed into a Harvard for the last time."

His Wings Test brought him next to the highest standing in the class, but his success wakened a fresh terror. Suppose "They" should decide that he should be used as an instructor? "Of all the horrible things that could happen, being kept in Canada to instruct for the rest of the War is the most horrible that could happen to any of us!"

7

"We are all through with everything now," he writes, a little prematurely, "and grounded, too, as they have the strange idea that, having won our Wings, we might be inclined to play around too much in the air!"

"They" are not too far wrong, and John nearly misses the actual bestowal of the Wings because of it.

"I'm beginning to think that I'm being preserved for something big by the Fates," he writes his brother David, "especially after what happened today. I went with another chap on a solo cross-country flight to Mount Hope, another E.P.T.S. in Ontario. All the way there we did rolls, loops, Immelmans, stall turns, etc., and had one magnificent dog-fight (strictly against orders!), finally arriving about three quarters of an hour later. Got a going-over from the C.O. there, and took off for home. I was ahead, so looped over him"—presumably his companion in the flight—"and sat on his tail, about 50 yards behind, pouring imaginary tracers into him like the devil.

"Suddenly, out of the blue, a Harvard (advanced trainer) dove down between us, just like a yellow blur. (They go about 200 to our 90.) The other chap went on home, but I stayed to grapple with the Harvard, despite the disadvantage of speed and manoeuvrability. Needless to say, he outflew me all the time, but, whenever I got him turning around me, I could turn inside him and drill him. Finally I saw him coming down on my tail again, so I half-rolled on to my back, and looped out, but held her in the dive till I had about 180 m.p.h. Pulled out at 500 feet, and, when my vision returned, he had already passed me and was circling a field. I circled inside but above him until he cut in and landed.

"After taking a good look around (we would be washed out on the spot if caught), I landed too and taxied over to him. He turned out to be a Flying Officer from Dunville, where we hope to get eventually, and complimented me on keeping him in my sights as long as I did. Finally he started off again.

"But there was a farmhouse at the windward corner of the field, so he decided to 'skim' it. This is another thing we are not allowed to do—that is, to fly low along the ground, then, almost in front of some fence, tree, etc., to yank back on the stick and zoom upwards at terrific speed. I did the same thing and, if he missed the house by five feet, I missed it by two. We climbed up and then dove on the unfortunate inmates again and again. Finally, I dipped my wings to him, thinking it was about time I got back. Besides, the ceiling was dropping rapidly and there was nasty looking weather to the N.W.

"Imagine my plight when, arriving back at the aerodrome, I was told to report to the Chief Flying Officer's office immediately. I went there, shivering in my boots, to face both the C.O. and the C.F.I."—the Chief Flying Instructor. "Apparently the poor benighted farmer had lodged a complaint against me (the Harvard was going too fast for him to get his number), and what could I say in my own defense? Of course it was useless to plead engine trouble, as they obviously knew I had been deliberately 'low-flying', the greatest crime you can commit in this outfit.

"I was quite open about it, told them about the whole thing, but refused to give the name of the Harvard pilot. Then the C.O. said he was probably going to wash me out, and went over to the Administration Building to see how I came out in our Ground School Finals, which had just been posted. I sat in silence with the C.F.I., who was just civil enough to offer me a cigarette.

"Almost 10 minutes later the C.O. came back into the room, slapped me on the back, and said 'Sorry, laddie, we haven't a hope of washing you out. You came in first!'

"This was really fantastic news as our subjects covered everything I've never been any good at—Aero engines, Armament, Navigation, Air-frame Construction, Theory of Flight, Signals, Morse, etc., most of which I thought I'd flunked, so I escaped with the skin of my teeth.

"His final words to me were: 'And for God's sake, remember that the crime is not in the doing, but in the getting caught!'"

And now the long period of training is at last over.

"I have never looked forward to coming home so much as I do now. Honestly, I can hardly wait to see you all again. The suspense of the last few weeks has been really terrific and I have lost a great deal of weight, and had no chance, to speak of, for exercise. I said I was grounded, but actually I have an hour's radio work to put in (formation flying by means of radio) and also I have a bet on with the Flight Commander that he can't make me sick in the course of an hour. I'm pretty sure to lose but it'll be good fun!"

In response to a letter in a Washington paper by his

brother Christopher, aged twelve, who is indignant because no one takes air-raid precautions seriously, John writes for once about the War. "I believe from what I am learning of aerial warfare that, if this war is over in two years, it will be the wrong way. Furthermore, I am convinced that the United States must not make the tragic mistake of France in saying 'It can't happen here'. All you have to do is transpose the Atlantic for the Maginot Line and you have what seems to me to be a very similar (almost ominously similar) situation. By all means, have your blackout practices. Practise, practise, practise, all the time for the worst. It may never happen, but *nobody* knows. Meanwhile, if you *expect* it, you are giving yourselves a little free life insurance. You can't know too much.

"I have no patience with the Americans who insist that they are safe behind the Atlantic. The fact that bombers are made now which can fly across the Atlantic and back with *thirty tons* of bombs may not mean anything to them, but they may live to rue the day when they failed to read their newspapers with foresight."

Then, once more, he is the upper ether's own play-boy. "I had fun this morning rolling through, looping around and circling a puffy little cloud."

8

Early in June, his Wings! The hollow square with the dark-uniformed students, standing at attention, bands, the brass-hats, solemn and proud, and the chief brass-hat, imported for the occasion, passing down the line, inspecting, making his speech and congratulating each flier as at last he pins the coveted emblem on the palpitating breast. So long a time between the medical examination at the Manning Pool and this little, yet so significant, gesture, so much hard work, so many aches and thrills, so much cold resolve and gritting of teeth, so much surrender of the self.

The Commanding Officer shakes John's hand and speaks a friendly word. John grins. Then leave . . . and home . . .

In the furnished house his parents had rented in Washington, other peoples' ancestors looked sternly down on a houseful of boys whose ebullient spirits threatened to blow the roof off. In one of his letters, John had expressed the hope that the household was running "with its usual tomb-like silence and Paradisian serenity". It was. David, next in line to John, was home from Hotchkiss, and Christopher and Hugh each had his own company of friends. The floors groaned and the walls shivered.

John, too, was in high feather, literally preening his Wings. The meager ten days of his leave seemed not half long enough for him to tell all he had to tell. The father, the mother, the four boys, clung to the minutes. Mephistoph-eles took the family into the lush countryside of Mary-

land and Virginia for occasional picnics, and John rough-
housed with his brothers as though a year had not passed
and they were all still children together on the beach at
East Chop. But the year had passed. David and Christopher insisted that John must give the capital's young men
a chance to learn about the R.C.A.F. and notified the
Washington papers that, on a certain evening, he would
hold an informal recruiting meeting. Some eighteen or
twenty young men showed up. John, in uniform, told them
the worst, and, in his own attractive person, was his own
most compelling argument for selfless service.

For the ego had really gone out of him. The discipline,
the danger, the fellowship of gallant men, the hunger to
perfect himself so that he might remain one of this high
company, had swept him clear of the softness, the selfconsciousness and the sophomoric cynicism. He was no
longer the restless, unsettled boy of the previous summer.
He had achieved something—something, indeed!—and he
knew at what cost; and stood upon that achievement with
assurance and matured power.

"It isn't necessarily the most dashing hero who makes
the best fighter pilot," he had written David a few weeks
before, and the words revealed how far he had gone. "It is
the man who knows his machine, knows his enemy and,
above all, *knows himself*. It is only by knowing the limita-
tions of all these that he can form any plan of attack."

They were the words of a man who had known the ordeal by fire.

John drove his father and his brothers to Pittsburgh to
say good-bye to his attractive relatives there, and emerged
from the visit with the announcement that he was engaged

to be married. His father thought he was joking. "Didn't you get what I said?" John persisted. "I said I was engaged."

The Czechoslovakian, it appeared, had been forgotten and a Pittsburgh beauty was now queen of his heart. His father refused to believe it, remembering a yet earlier devotion, and John, junior, could not even make the young lady's name stick in his memory.

And then they are back in Washington with only forty-eight hours, twenty-four, eighteen, twelve, before he must take the plane to the Canadian port of embarkation. The parents grant one of the remaining hours to a young Washington lawyer, John Stigall, himself something of a poet, who has read John's little book and the yet unprinted "Brave New World", and is determined to see him before he goes. There is lively talk of poetry, and of John's future as a poet.

John is not at all convinced that he has a future. He has written one poem, possibly two, since his coming to America. Perhaps his poetry has been nothing but the fitful flowering of adolescence. He may never write again.

The older man protests. John *has* something, something to be nourished and allowed to grow, a talent, perhaps even a touch of genius. . . . John kindles. Perhaps . . . perhaps . . .

His new friend departs and John is alone with his father and mother. They sit, talking, until long after midnight. They have so much to catch up on, so much to say that they will be unable to say tomorrow and on so many tomorrows to follow.

His father and mother are conscious that they are no longer talking to a boy, but to a man, and speak of precious, intimate things, of love and marriage, and growth in love through the sharing of joy and trouble in the outwardly unromantic routine of living, set aglow by the Presence of God. John speaks of Foxburrow, the house he loves on the shore at Kingsdown. If, by a miracle, Diana should be willing to marry him, might they have the house for whatever brief honeymoon might be permitted them?

John is troubled about the question of hate. Is it ever right for a Christian to hate his enemy in war? "I'm afraid, if I don't hate him," he says, "that his bullets will get me before mine get him."

Through the hours of the hot June night, with the dissonance of the trolley-wheels making the bend under the bronze eyes of General McClellan, unreal and of another world, father and mother and son experience the perfect fellowship of understanding, at rest in love and faith.

And, at last, they are all three on their knees. . . .

John was having a late breakfast next morning with his father when the door-bell rang and the colored maid handed him a telegram. He let out a yell that cut through three stories and startled the pigeons on the roof. A window next door was flung open and the colored maid called to Daisy, the Magees' cook, asking who had been murdered.

John waved the yellow sheet. The impossible had happened, the prize he imagined he had forfeited by his bad luck, or his follies, was his. In sober bureaucratic language he was informed that he had been gazetted as an officer, as from a date two weeks previous.

There was no room for any sadness of farewell on top of that, certainly not for John and scarcely for his parents. At the airport they watched the plane that took him northward become first a hawk, then a sparrow, then a fly in the June sky, and their hearts were so full of thankfulness for the man who yesterday had been a boy that they had no room for sorrow or apprehension.

9

John is back in Montreal, getting fitted for his new uniform. "I was saluted this morning for the first time by an army corporal," he writes. "He was rather taken aback when I rushed up and grabbed him by the hand and congratulated him on being the first man ever to salute my undistinguished self."

A long slow passage across the Atlantic, very roundabout, very tedious, very uncomfortable, and, at last, hope deferred becomes hope fulfilled and he is in England. "There is, I find, some truth in the saying, 'Join the Army and see the world'," he writes a friend, "(though, as I write, I can't help remembering a similar exhortation to 'Join the Air Force and see the Next!')." The censor does his worst with the letter describing the journey but permits him to reveal that "after a long and tedious train journey, in which we sat up twenty-four hours in a very cramped position (I slept on a luggage-rack until it broke) we arrived at the Personnel Reception Center and were put up in a magnificent hotel for about a week, much to our astonishment." He is sent to a training camp in South Wales for final training before joining his squadron.

"The first day I got here I revolted," he writes his family, "and took a day off to go and find Diana, whom I found buried in the Gloucestershire Hills not very far away and looking lovelier than ever."

He had dreamed of that return for two long years.

135

"I know, dear heart, that some day I shall find you
   Alone, and in the evening shade of trees;
Twilight, and hills, and quietness behind you
   —A scent I shall remember in the breeze. . . .

"Always you come, a precious ghost, to haunt
   The days, the nights; in sudden, waking dreams
I find your face; you smile, you beckon, flaunt
   Your lovely self before my eyes. It seems

"To love is pain! But did you really care?
   Have you forgotten? Is it all in vain
To breathe out sonnets to the midnight air,
   To long to touch your hands, your lips again?

"And yet, I know that some day I shall find you
   Alone, and in the evening shade of trees;
Twilight, and hills, and quietness behind you
   —A scent I shall remember in the breeze. . . ."

Hugh Lyon and his attractive family were staying with
friends for the fruit-picking season. John came by plane and
terrified the sleepy little village as he zoomed close over it
before turning for his landing. "It was a joy to us all to see
him," wrote the headmaster afterward.

Diana, who was staying with the Lyons, watched him
with her mature and penetrating eyes, to see what the two
years in America had done to the youth she had known, the
shy boy who took life so seriously, yet had so light-hearted
an aptitude for doing "funny things". She had never been
quite sure how serious his love-making was. He seemed to

live in a dream-world, inhabited by a fanciful Diana, as unreal as himself, and had been inclined to be sorry for him,
hoping he would grow out of it, since she was fond of him,
but not as he wanted her to be. He was more mature, she
could see; he had more self-confidence and much better
manners. He had always been "a very interesting person to
talk to," she wrote subsequently, "because, being a poet with
a sense of humor, he could understand things very well. In
his letters he had sometimes spoken seriously of the war,
and of his feelings about it, but, although he said once that
war seemed utterly foolish, he was obviously longing to do
the foolish thing and join in the fighting as soon as possible. I found he was just like his letters, full of life and
ready to enjoy everything that happened to him, pleasant
or not, and hardly ever talking about his own feelings."

He stayed four hours and was back again next morning
for breakfast, and overhead again next day, doing aerobatics
to the anguish and delight of the villagers and of the Lyon
family and Diana. "He nearly took our chimneys off in his
Spitfire", she wrote. When, shortly after, a deluge of rain
grounded all planes, "he braved the most uncomfortable
and lengthy train journey," wrote the headmaster, "to spend
a few hours with the family that loved him."

He gave Hugh Lyon the impression of being "on top of
the world", one who had found the life for which he was
made and "went to it in the full and almost joyful knowledge of the hazards which went with it—especially to one
who, like himself, did not know the meaning of 'safety
first'. All the poet and all the adventurer in him found expression and outlet in the Air Force."

"Had a marvellous time," John wrote home, "walking

over the hills, working in the fields, and eating my head off."

"We walked on Bredon Hill one evening," Diana reported, "(and in spite of his moustache John only looked about fifteen when he was out of uniform) and I think it made him happy to see England again, for we talked very cheerfully and raced each other downhill."

Even a final training camp is a bit tame after anything like that, especially in the rain, which is constant, the Welsh hills holding the clouds captive day after day. The lanes are knee-deep in water, which means something when you have to walk half a mile to the bath-hut, a little farther to the mess and a mile or so more to the flying field. Yet, John writes, "I am happy here, though our living conditions aren't particularly luxurious."

The base has its compensations and he admits in a letter to friends that he is having "a wonderful time. The officers' mess is about the loudest, gayest place I have ever hit. Whenever anybody so much as scratches a plane he has to buy drinks all round. If he is in hospital or the mortuary it goes on his Mess Bill, which he'll never have to pay anyway."

Nevertheless, he seeks the upper air at every opportunity and growls when he is grounded because he is away ahead in flying time of anyone else in "A" flight to which he is attached. "Every time I go up," he explains, "I can't bear to come down while I have any gas left." For he is completely in love with the plane he is given to fly. "I could rhapsodize for pages about the Spitfire. It is a thrilling and at the same time terrifying aircraft. It takes off so quickly that before you have recovered from the shock you are sitting pretty at 5,000 feet!"

"If we get a nice day (that is, with cloud cover)," he writes, "a bunch of us are going to run across to the French Coast and back, in the hope of finding something small and badly armoured to initiate ourselves on! Of course, there is no telling what we will make of ourselves in this great game we have gone into. Few of us, I imagine, have any ideas as to what may lie ahead. Personally, though, I feel a certain inexpressible thrill and ecstasy at the prospect of operations. I also have that feeling which I call dentist tummy—my mouth goes dry, hands clammy, and my knees feel as if they are about to give way. Then it passes, and once again I am looking forward to it."

After a month in Britain, he finds the flying "as marvellous as the weather is atrocious. . . . The other day I was lucky enough to get a Spit without any squadron markings on it, so I could fly as low as I liked and not get turned in. First of all, I beat up the Lyons for about three-quarters of an hour, almost touching the grass on the tennis court several times. After that, I shot off to S—— and beat up Dermott"—an old friend—"then down to Mortehoe to have a look at Granny. Unfortunately, at the top of the hill I misjudged a pull-out and left some elevator fabric on a bramble bush. Must have given her quite a thrill, but it took some explaining back here.

"Yesterday we had our first air-raid warning, but the 'all clear' came about ten minutes later. Yesterday, also, I led a flight formation up through cloud (quite hard). We stayed up for about an hour and then came down through a hole in the clouds, but when we arrived back here we found cloud right down to the deck. We were all lucky to get in without mishap. We did some camera-gun attacks the other day, the results of which encouraged me very much, as I was the only person in the whole course who had the 'enemy' plane on the film for more than half the length. It was not particularly steady, but the aim and range were good. I am going to concentrate like mad on my shooting, as this is obviously what counts.

"I shall be joining a squadron just about the time you get this, I imagine. I am trying to get into a good Canadian squadron 'resting up', in the North Country. This is the best time to join a squadron, as they have a chance to mould you into the scheme of things and you have a chance to practice, practice, practice, so that, when the squadron moves south again, you are (theoretically) red hot . . .

"Today the sun is shining for the first time since we came here. And I can't fly because I am too far ahead of the others. The irony of life!"

By the middle of September, John had completed his final training and was ready for combat. For a day or two he was in London, a day or two in Rugby, then Lincolnshire and the Squadron. His arrival was suitably celebrated. "It was most warming (actually not so much a compliment as I thought, as any excuse for a party is good enough)."

"I have spent all day today dogfighting," he writes a day or two later, "and feel most exhausted. Most of it was at 20,000 feet, where oxygen is needed. I felt like Icarus about to singe his wings. Incidentally, I have been as high as 33,000 feet. Higher than the top of Mt. Everest!"—and eight months before he had written of the "tremendous height of 6500 feet!" "I have about thirty hours on Spitfires now, and expect to be through this course in a week, if the rain keeps off.

"The following is a list of fighter slang which you may find creeping into my letters:

(1) Prang	Crack-up.
(2) Operational	(a) Good, efficient, active.
Fully Operational	(b) Becoming to an airman, e. g., My hat is becoming sufficiently battered to be called "Operational".
(3) Had it	(a) Had the short end of the stick, dirty deal, or got into trouble. If a man damages an aircraft,—
	(b) "He's had it." Also means "I've had this lunch," i. e. "Am fed up with same."
(4) Pulpit or Office	Cockpit
(5) Hunted Bird	Pilot
(6) Dice ⎫ i. e. with Death Flirt ⎭	Fly

"I can't think of any more at the moment.

"I am enclosing a verse ["High Flight"] I wrote the other day. It started at 30,000 feet, and was finished soon after I landed. I thought it might interest you.

"Diana has had a novelette accepted by somebody or other, about which she is very excited. I go over where they are staying"—meaning presumably high over—"practically every day, but of late I have been spending most of my time in formation and air combat.

"My squadron contains surely the grandest bunch of peo-

ple that ever lived. I am sure I am going to be very happy
here. I was rather apprehensive on first coming here, lest
they should not turn out to be good fellows, as these, I
realized, would be the chaps I shall be living, eating, laughing, and fighting with for the duration. It is an all-Canadian
squadron, recently formed. I am glad it is a young squadron,
as the newcomer immediately becomes 'one of the boys',
instead of having to serve a term of virtual apprenticeship.
For the first few weeks here I shall not be doing an awful
lot.

"The squadron leader is a peach, quiet but efficient and
thoughtful. He is taking half the squadron south next week
to go on sweeps for a few days. I wish I were going, but,
of course, I am only small fry as yet!

"When we get really hot," John writes his Aunt Mary, "we
shall undoubtedly be moved down to the real theatre of
operations—the southeast Coast. At the moment, we are
supposed to be defending the North-Eastern approaches.
Occasionally we find a ship to shoot up to relieve the mo-
notony of the coastal patrols at dawn and dusk. I expect to
be going on the next sweep, though I shall be flying 'in the
box' i. e. 'boxed' in by the more experienced fellows.

"Last time our squadron went, they ran into a hive of
activity in which about 700 Spitfires, Hurrybirds and 109's
were involved.

"One fellow, flying 'in the box' on this, his first en-
gagement with the enemy, got separated from the squadron
when they positioned for attack and later found himself
flying, as he thought West, but actually East, as his com-
pass needle was stuck. After a while, two other 'Spitfires'
joined him and flew in very close formation on him. For a

few minutes he took a look at them and, in his own words
. . . 'the only thing I remember thinking was how beautiful they looked in their dazzling new camouflage, and I was
just wondering what squadron they belonged to when I
felt my body freeze completely. They weren't Spitfires at
all, but Messerschmitt 109's. There was no room for either
of us to get our guns to bear, and anyway I think the pilots
must have had a sense of humor, as they both took off their
oxygen masks and grinned at me . . . one thumbed his
nose. Just then it occurred to me that I was flying *into Germany* and had only about 20 gallons of gas left, and I suddenly feared that this might be some sort of trap, so I half
rolled and dove away from between those 109's' . . . (This
is an extract of his report.)

"Actually, to cut a long story short, he ran out of gas
halfway over the Channel but managed to stay in his plane
until he had glided within reach of the English Coast, then
baled out from 1,000 feet (this is very low) and landed on
the edge of the cliffs about three and a half miles south of
Foxburrow.

"Everybody says the same thing about the Messerschmitts—they are so beautiful that quite frequently it
never occurs to the fledgling to fire his guns at them!"

Meanwhile, at the station, life goes on in a fashion which
to John is distressingly humdrum for an arm of the service
basically so romantic. "We live in the most informal manner," he writes his father and mother. "Although it is a
permanent R.A.F. station (pre-war, that is), we meander
about, even in the Mess, in battle dress and flying boots,
sweaters, etc., much to the disgust of some of the more
dignified 'penguins' (non-flying officers) and brown types

(army officers) here." They play cards daily for the use of a light plane, the winner taking it for a day or a week-end. A and B flights—John is in A—interchange as dawn and dusk patrols.

"Although we get a certain amount of practice flying (in air combat, air-to-air firing, air-to-ground firing, air-to-sea firing, formation attacks, practice 'scrambles', etc.) most of our time is spent waiting for a Scramble in the dispersal hut, where I am now writing. We sit here all day and get very bored." In a Scramble, it seems, the fliers rush out to the planes, whose ground crews, seeing the fliers coming, have started the engines, "slip into their parachutes, which will be left dangling from a wing-tip, throw on their hel-mets and oxygen masks, fall somehow into the 'office' and take off in any old direction, form up in the air, and they're away. Meanwhile, those who are on '15 minutes' will be getting ready for their Scramble to come through, and those on '30 minutes' for theirs. Some of these might be in bed, or away eating, or trap shooting, good practice for air fir-ing,—anywhere, as long as they can be airborne in the allotted time. This happens rather too seldom, though!

"We often spend all day just waiting, which is a little trying on the nerves. Luckily, I brought a good many books with me from Rugby (where I found, to my immense pleas-ure, that I had some credit left at a book shop—remains of the Poem Prize), and I also bought some model aeroplane kits at Hamleys, which make a good pastime. One of the essential things in a squadron is to keep occupied. Some of the boys do the most amazing things. Can you imagine a fighter pilot knitting?!!!"

John, being an officer, had an orderly, called in Britain a

"batman", a sawed-off Britisher with a shrewd eye, who subsequently gave his impressions. "The first time I met P/O J. Magee I thought to myself what a sissy what have they given me now. I called him Longfellow Magee so did the other members of the staff. Had a nasty habit of throwing his things about, very hard to wake up, boy shake him I used to, call him all things behind his back but still we got on well. I could talk to him as though I was talking to my own pal. As time wore on he changed sir believe me sir he changed. The R.C.A.F. made a man out of him and if it comes to that so did England. He was very thoughtful towards me in fact too thoughtful. I could never do anything for him unless he said you need not have bothered it was okay what do you ask for have a rest take it easy. What you panicking for?

"I was not allowed to call him sir many a time and believe me sir that was one of the main things that got me to like J. Magee.

"The men of 412 liked him sir as much as I did, his ways, his manner, his work, and his cooperation with the men. He was a grand flier, crazy on flying, plenty of guts, and believe me sir he lived up to his nationality."

So, fitting himself into the new fellowship P/O J. Magee learns and grows.

"I have recently taken myself to task for being too apt to show my emotions," he writes his mother, "and have since developed a sharp distaste for any emotional display—other, perhaps, than that of anger, which, being a weak point of mine, I am apt to be inconsistent about! Over here, though, you begin to appreciate the pettiness of emotion displayed. We live under a pretty good nervous strain and yet there have been a good many instances of even righteous wrath well kept under control. Several times there have been minor adjustments overlooked on aircraft which might have caused an unnecessary fatality, yet I have very seldom heard anyone blow up at his fitter or rigger on such a score."

Yes, Johnny Magee was growing up.

"The glimpses he gave in his talk and in his poetry of the restless, questioning spirit which lay behind both his religious awareness and his occasional escapades," wrote Hugh Lyon after his death, "always gave promise of that wise maturity which was never to be his. But somehow I couldn't ever think of him as mature; he had the flash of youth as something inherent in him, the swift adventurous response to any challenge, which I hated to think might ever die down into the steady lukewarm glow of middle age."

Paul Child, John's thoughtful and imaginative mentor at Avon, was no less assured of the fruitful maturity that might have lain ahead.

"I feel certain that, if there had been more time in his life, he would gradually have coalesced the disparate elements which made the complicated, but as yet uncrystallized, person we knew. The tortuous swinging of the religious pendulum and the wild struggle of his aesthetic sensibilities against the prison walls of facts and figures, would have reached a more stable and productive rhythm from which some splendid masterpiece might have emerged."

10

The Squadron goes south on "an army cooperation job", John writes, consisting "almost exclusively of beating up tanks, gunposts, artillery, troops, etc. in low level attacks during a big army manoeuvre. Of course it was all pretense but gave us some good experience and, besides, it was wonderful fun and we had a bellyful of thrills. We were shifted about all over the place during the week we were there; in fact, we were never more than 36 hours in one place. We started out not far from Rugby and gradually retreated with the defending forces in a southeasterly direction in the face of a terrific 'enemy' onslaught. It was quite a job, each move an agony of demolishing and rebuilding encampments, trying to put up tents, etc."

The festivities, when the expedition is over, are something to remember.

"The Winco (Wing-Commander)," John writes his Aunt Mary, "thought we ought to have a party to celebrate our efforts for the Army. Accordingly, tunics were thrown off, collars loosened, and the Officer's Mess started to disintegrate. The poor W.A.A.F.S.—Woman's Auxiliary Air Force Service—who serve at the bar, never had a moment's peace, because, when a whole Canadian Wing (3 squadrons) decides to have a party, you know all about it!

"At four in the morning we were playing some roughhouse game where people were literally being hurled through the air and caught the other side of the room. The proceedings ended when I inadvertently pushed my Squadron Leader into the fire-place and the Station Adjutant landed on his head on the floor, having been missed by the 412th Sqdn. Intelligence Officer, who was supposed to catch him! We (all 50 of us) carried him up to bed in a coma and then retired ourselves. Dawn patrol the next day was an awe-inspiring exhibition. Certainly we flew the straggliest formation that has ever been seen hereabouts, and one of our Flight-Lieuts. landed in a tree."

By the middle of October, John is on combat duty, having been "on several operations against the enemy already, but I think I had better not say much about these. Eddie M——, a sergeant pilot in 412, got his, and the Squadron's, first confirmed victory on an offensive sweep the other day. It was a Messerschmitt 109E. It, of course, called for a tremendous party, which in no way improved our sensory faculties for the following day's operations.

"Today I was to have gone on a sweep, but the weather, as usual, prevented our taking part. I went on my first 'Scramble' some days ago, in other words, I was on 'readiness' with one other pilot when the loudspeaker crackled and we left in a hurry, hardly waiting to hear what the controller said. We went away out into the North Sea, just one section (i. e. two planes) in search of a Junker-88, but unfortunately got into some excessively bad weather and couldn't find him.

"Another rather exciting operation involved low flying just over the top of the water practically all the way to Holland. The whole squadron was in formation and it must have looked pretty formidable to any who might have been watching from some of the naval ships we passed over" . . .

"Recently, I have been acting as Test Pilot for the squadron. We have one old kite that is in the last stages of decrepitude, which nobody likes to fly. It had a thorough overhaul but they didn't manage to get the wheels quite right, so, in a rash moment, I volunteered to air-test it. Everything went all right until I came in for a landing, and then the wheels wouldn't come down. The only thing you can do in such a case is to go through a series of short dives and violent pull-outs, which is pretty hard on the pilot and *very* hard on the wings!

"I went round and round the aerodrome very low doing this until I thought the wings would come off, but still they"—presumably the wheels—"wouldn't come down. I was almost ready to crash-land it, with the wheels retracted, when I decided to have one more go. I got up to about 2,000 feet (I couldn't get it to climb properly as the engine was not running at all well), rolled onto my back and chopped vertically onto the aerodrome. I held it as long as I dared—and a little longer—then hauled the stick back into my stomach as hard as I could. All I remember before blacking out was a very violent jerk and shudder which I mentally noted as the disappearance of the wings (a most essential part of any aeroplane!) but when I came to again my impressions were chronologically as follows:

I. The wings are here

II. The wheels are down

III. I am about to hit a hangar.

However, I finally got down safely. On taxiing up to the

flight officer I found—you'll never guess—the Duke of Kent inspecting the squadron. My Flight Commander introduced me and said 'Nice work' which I took as an enormous compliment, as he is not exactly given to flattery. The Duke had watched the whole procedure and seemed duly impressed.

"Today I tested the same aircraft again. The mechanic had been onto it and guaranteed that it would work, so I took off gaily in the direction of my old school"—he is referring to Rugby—"which I duly found, and, the plane having no markings on it (it had just been repainted), proceeded to give the old place a really good 'beating up'. I had fleeting impressions of boys pouring out of class-rooms; Barbara Lyon waving a blue handkerchief; Eric Reynolds standing aghast by his bicycle; and that hideous monstrosity, the school chapel.

"Having arrived back at the aerodrome I found once more that the wheels stuck. So, mouthing words at the flight mechanic, I started to go through the same manoeuvres as before. This time I had a little more height and could afford to be more violent. After 45 *minutes* I got them down at the expense of two engine cowlings, the hood and several bolts out of the wing-roots which all shook off in the process. I have just told the engineering officer that next time I'm going to bail out and let it fall into the sea!

"I don't know why I should have spent two pages, telling you of such a mundane article as an undercart, but news is rather scarce.

"P.S. I have decided to be a flying instructor after the war. If it looks like ending suddenly, please get me a job at once!

"P.P.S. I like flying."

11

The end of October brings a seven days' leave, and he makes the most of it. London . . . Oxford . . . supper with Diana, who is a student at Lady Margaret Hall, and his friend, Dermott Magill, studying at Oriel. "I attended a lecture with Dermott and his room-mate, suitably attired in sports coat, *very* loud canary jersey, and gown! It was a lecture on Goethe and I was terrified that the man would ask me a question. However, he didn't."

He climbs back into his uniform and assails the fastnesses of Lady Margaret Hall for tea with Diana.

"I eventually found her room, after butting in on all sorts of other young ladies. I had been so excited to receive the invitation on the previous evening that I had completely forgotten what number she said. Dermott assured me it was T 23; I was equally certain it was H 58; actually it was D 31! Tea went off very well. I think I am making a bit of headway, but of course it may be the uniform. After that, Dermott, his room-mate and I invited Diana and two of her friends to see a play called 'The Blue Goose' which, as I remember it, was rather poor, but I was not paying much attention, as Diana and I were conversing most of the time. Then we had supper at a restaurant and walked the girls back to L.M.H. (they had to be in at 11.15). On the way, one of the other girls walked with me, but Diana rather skillfully edged her out by stumbling more or less between us. I would give my eyes to know if that stumble was really an accident!"

Love, and the poet's eye for beauty, conspired to make Oxford glow in his eyes. "I had never, I think, been to Oxford before. It is, without a doubt, the most beautiful city I have ever visited. It also has an air of peace and learning which I don't find at any of the American universities I have been to (not to the same extent, anyway). I would certainly like to go there after the war, but I suppose it would be silly to waste that Yale scholarship.

"However, I think that if I go to college in America my life will be in that country, whereas my heart is still here! And the fact that that young lady is showing just the very faintest signs of relenting does not encourage me to leave it! Now that I have a motorbike"—he had bought it, a little guiltily, on the instalment plan, and been granted a license after a single attempt to drive—"I ought to be able to get down to see Diana more often. She has really turned out to be the most inspiring girl. I enjoy her company more now than ever before. . . . Really I think she must be the girl for me. But I foresee years of hard work before I win her heart! Any advice," he added, "will be gratefully received."

"In spite of a pipe and the moustache," Diana wrote, giving her own account of the Oxford weekend, "he still seemed extraordinarily young. It was impossible to imagine him any older. He was enjoying life more than ever, and combined a genuine hatred of war with intense enjoyment of the excitement it provided and a desire to do some real fighting. He spoke once of what he wanted to be after the war, and seemed eager to go to either Oxford or Cambridge, and finish his education, but his thoughts were more of the present and I think he was too interested in his part in the war to plan for the time afterwards."

He visited his grandmother at Mortehoe in North Devon; Mortehoe, where he had spent his memorable Easter vacation two years before and, standing on Morte Hill with Geoffrey Sergeant, had seen visions and dreamed dreams. It was with his mother's sister that this time he climbed the hill to St. Mary's church where he had taken the Holy Communion with Geoffrey, his Aunt Ruth, who had spent her life in self-abnegating service of others and had mothered him during the years his own mother was in China. John had always considered her rather forbidding, and found her now "a great lady"—with "a sort of air about her which exhales patience, wisdom and unselfishness." His tribute was a fresh indication that John was growing up. They walked together into the old church, where, John noted, he was "the object of much attention and speculation by a small girls' school there (I have a new uniform now, which is a great deal better than the old one!").

After luncheon he walked out to Morte Point, the scene of his memorable sessions with Geoffrey Sergeant, wooing this time not abstract Truth but, pencil and paper in hand, the muse. He found her "absolutely sterile. So I took to watching gulls, but they all seemed to be crying 'Diana! Diana!', and her face was everywhere, so, in the end, I got fed up and came back to tea."

Yes, he was in love.

Here Diana picks up the story. "Before he went back to the squadron he came to say good-bye, and brought an old motor-bicycle he had acquired. It was just like him, I thought, to buy a cycle that kept breaking down and had to be pushed most of the time, and it caused him great amusement by its eccentricities.

"We shook hands rather solemnly, when he went, and it seemed rather foolish and inadequate to wish him 'good luck', because, whatever happened, he considered himself marvellously lucky, and I never remember him complaining of anything.

"The motor-bike, however, cheered us up a bit; it went five yards and then stopped dead, and, when at last it went on again, we laughed and John waved his hand and disappeared round the corner."

12

"*November 10, 1941.* I have at last been in action. November 8th I shall never forget. I can't tell you much about it, but it took place in enemy territory. I was flying in the leading section of four as the C.O.'s wing man. We were jumped and I was the only one to avoid getting hit. The C.O., who used to be my Flight Commander, a Pilot Officer, and our best sergeant were all shot down. I arrived back in England with a couple of Poles at a town about 15 miles south of our home, which, by the way, seemed O.K. from the air.

"I had a crack at a Jerry but didn't see any results, so am not claiming it. The Mess has an air of forced cheerfulness just now. Our losses (the first we have sustained) were pretty hard to take, but we needed some waking up. Everyone is determined to get something next time.

"The censors are getting very strict and I have told you only what was in the papers. The rest is a long story and must keep till I get home. I was completely terrified throughout but hope not to be so next time."

Another letter, undated, gave further details of his first baptism of fire. "The 109's," he wrote, "came down in swarms out of the sun. I was terrified at first but, after a while, felt a bit better and had a squirt at one, but another was firing at me so I didn't see whether I hit him or not. Kitt B——, who used to be "A" Flight Commander, had been made a Squadron Leader and took over T——'s place.

He had only had his stripes up for one day when he led the Squadron, and was shot down. I was the last man to see him alive, as, just before we took off, he was giving me a little fatherly advice, as it was my first action and I was a little uneasy. I flew as his wing man.

"We were jumped by four 109's who picked one of us each. We all turned into them immediately, but I turned so violently that I spun down a good many thousand feet and got away. The other three were all shot down. I saw D—— go straight into the sea. P—— tried to bail out, but his parachute didn't open. Nobody saw what happened to Kitt, but we all think and hope he is a prisoner of war. He was one of the grandest men I have ever known.

"It was when I was way below the others that I got my squirt. A 109 was following somebody down, firing intermittently, and all I had to do was turn in behind and fire at him, but another one pulled the same trick on me, and, when I saw tracers going by, it was time to forget about my bird, who, I think, must have got it as he was a sitting target for me. However, I couldn't claim him, as I didn't see him go in.

"I have described what happened on one sweep. We shall be doing more and more of these in the future. Once you get over your fear at the 109's you get to love it. We are also doing low flying cannon attacks on aerodromes, power plants, and other such targets. They're great fun but the anti-aircraft fire is a little disconcerting at first. . . .

"Really, I am loving the whole thing. Incidentally, when we go on these operations across the Channel we usually fly down as a Squadron . . . After the sweep on the 8th (my first) I landed at ——. but everyone was sent back again to look for survivors in the sea. It was dark when I got back and I spent the night there and then flew back here"—the aerodrome in Lincolnshire—"the following morning, feeling rather enervated. I passed very low over Foxburrow which seemed to be intact. On these sweeps you go over as a Squadron, but you invariably get split up and dribble back in two's and three's and land at the first aerodrome you can find."

He sent his family what he called "another trifle which may interest you", an obscure first draft of sombre stanzas not yet integrated into a poem, reaching out hungrily for the support of the heroic dead. "I am not particularly anxious to have it printed," he added, "*unless* you think it vital to the conduct of hostilities! Seriously, though, do use it for any purposes such as War Relief, etc."

He called the poem "Per Ardua" (*Per ardua ad astra* was the motto of the Royal Canadian Air Force) and set under the title the following:

> "To those who gave their lives to England during the
> Battle of Britain and left such a shining example to us
> who follow, these lines are dedicated."

"They that have climbed the white mists of the morning,
   They that have soared before the world's awake,
To herald up their foeman to them, scorning
   The thin dawn's rest their weary folk might take.

"Some that left other mouths to tell the story
   Of high, blue battle, quite young limbs that bled,
How they had thundered up the clouds to glory,
   Or fallen to an English field stained red.

"*Because my faltering feet would fail I find them*
  Laughing beside me, steadying the hand
That seeks their deadly courage—
                    Yet behind them
The cold light dies in that once brilliant Land. . . .

"*Do these, who help the quickened pulse run slowly,*
  Whose stern, remembered image cools the brow,
Till the far dawn of Victory, know only
  Night's darkness, and Valhalla's silence now?"

For a moment the old doubt—the theme of so many midnight discussions with Larry Viles—comes surging back—
"What hope is there that I shall live again?"

November passed in breathless adventure.

"Really, you have no idea," John wrote Larry, "how terrifying—and yet how marvellous—it all is. I am determined to get a 'confirmed' "—an enemy plane whose loss is confirmed by his superiors—"before Christmas.

"We are expecting to move to a sphere of greater activity in a few days. However, while up here, we have done a lot of night flying and are well on the way to becoming night operational, so we'll be having two chances every day to build up a score and it shouldn't take long.

"The squadron contains a hell of a good bunch of fellows. Our mess at the moment is an old country cottage in a village about five miles from the aerodrome—the sort of place where you bump your head everywhere you go. I have never had such fun in my life. Frankly, however, I do not expect to last. It's not a very sensible thing to talk about, on the whole, but, to be good, you've got to take chances and you can't win all the time. Anyway, I'd rather be good. The ordinary world seems a long way away and unbearably dull and I can't say that I have a lot of ambition to go back to it under the same circumstances." . . . "So it is," he wrote another friend, "that I expect to end my days here in England, and it suits me down to the ground." He would like to build up "a score" and perhaps get a "bong", a decoration, though that is secondary, though it would help to justify his existence. But the old round . . . no . . . not while there are "high blue days" over England and the surrounding sea.

"He liked to live at full speed," Diana wrote afterwards, "and danger only made life more thrilling. I don't think he could have borne to grow old." She ended with a paradox. "I think he had found out how to live, and loved being alive so much that I think he could not have been afraid of death."

"Our squadron has lost rather heavily of late," John writes Robert Dawson, a schoolmate of his St. Clare days, "and we have had three squadron leaders in the last month. I have been in it only three and a half months and, as it is, I am one of its oldest members. Kitt Bushell, who was our best C.O., was shot down with three other fellows. . . . It is indeed a weird and chilly thing to see someone you know and live with go down in smoke. You can see all the 'Dawn Patrols' and 'Hell's Angels' you like but it isn't the same thing. And, too, it gets you kind of mad."

The casual and the romantic jostle elbows through the days. "I am becoming a squash enthusiast. 'Dusty' D—— and I play regularly when the weather permits (i. e. is bad!)

which is fortunately or unfortunately (I forget which) pretty frequent. I am certainly determined to survive this winter, despite the fog and general dampness!" "My decrepit motor bike (the light of my life) is on its last legs already." He raffles it off to the highest bidder, forgetting entirely that he still owes ten pounds on it. "Did I tell you that the King came down the other day? There were pictures in all the papers. . . . Exercising a great deal of imagination you can pick me out." . . . "I am well on the way to being night-operational. As soon as we have two dozen pilots night-operational, we will be allowed to take part in night-flying activities too. . . . You must imagine me doing a little more as the weeks go by (it's all a matter of experience) and, incidentally, having the time of my life."

"We have been moderately inactive just recently," John wrote his Aunt Mary early in December, "partly because of the weather and partly because the Hun is showing at present a marked distaste for English travelling this winter and we have to go out and look for him. At present I am a section-leader which means that I lead three other men in the air. I am also second in command of my flight (or have been acting as such during the last two weeks, as one of our fellows is sick and does not seem to be getting much better). There are two flights in a squadron.

"We are taking advantage of this lack of gumption that the Hun is exhibiting to get back at him on his own side of the water. I have been to see him several times now, and we have left visiting cards more than once. Generally speaking, though, there is not a great deal doing, but we are getting pretty hard by constant exercise and much fresh air and all the practice combat flying we can get in. I am better than I ever was, despite the fact that we have a minor bust-up practically every night. Today two of our sergeants received their commissions and are moving into the Officer's Mess, so I foresee a major operation ahead this evening. In spite of these frequent big nights we are frequently up at 7 to fly, as, when we get a good day, we take advantage of it.

"You offer kindly in your letter to act as my agent for anything else I write. It is very kind of you, but I assure you that there will not be any more!"

Several years before, he had written a "Prayer", which, with a boy's sentimental melancholy, anticipated the moment in which, unknowingly, he was now standing.

"Some evening, when I'm sitting out alone
Watching, perhaps, a cloud across the sky,
I'll feel as if a strange cool wind has blown—
And suddenly I'll know that I'm to die;

"Then I'll remember how we stood together,
And laughed, and kissed the lovely sun to bed;
And how we talked of Death among the heather,
And wondered gaily at the Ancient Dead. . . .

"When breath comes short, and tears come all in vain,
And in the silence I must realize
That I shall never laugh, nor love again,
May I find, leaning over me,—your eyes."

He telephoned his old headmaster of St. Clare, for he liked to keep in touch with old friends. "It was the same John we had known as a boy of twelve, when he might be laughing and crying almost in the same breath . . . the same eagerness, the same excited lilt in his voice . . ."

On a brief furlough, he went once more to Rugby to see the Lyons. "He arrived late one night," the headmaster remembered afterward, "and, just before he went back the next afternoon, he came and talked a little to me as I was sawing wood in my garage. It was good of him to come round, for he was in a hurry. He spoke a little about my family, a little about the prospects of going abroad, but not much about anything. It wasn't necessary somehow. 'So in all love we parted.' After he had gone, I went on sawing, and thinking of him, and the fine man he was growing up to be."

"WHERE NEVER LARK . . ."

"Oh! I have slipped the surly bonds of Earth
  And danced the skies on laughter-silvered wings;
Sunward I've climbed, and joined the tumbling mirth
  Of sun-split clouds. . . ."

"Before receipt of this letter you will have received notification from the Air Ministry of the sad loss you have sustained in the passing of your son John.

"It was during local practice manoeuvres that your son met with the accident causing his death, his plane colliding with another machine when emerging from a cloud, both machines crashing.

"Your son's funeral took place at Scopwick Cemetery, near Digby Aerodrome, at 2:30 P. M. on Saturday, 13th December, 1941, the service being conducted by Flight Lieutenant S. K. Belton, the Canadian padre of this Station. He was accorded full Service Honors, the coffin being carried by pilots of his own Squadron.

"Wreaths were sent by his brother officers, and airmen of his Squadron, also from the Royal Air Force Station, Digby. His grave will be taken care of by the Imperial War Graves Commission, who will erect a temporary wooden cross pending the provision of a permanent memorial.

"I would like to express the great sympathy I and all members of 412 Squadron feel with you in the loss of your son. John was a very popular member of our Squadron, which, as well as being an operational unit, is also a compact family of its own, and can ill afford to lose so valued a member as your son. He was held in very high regard both as a fighter pilot and a good friend of all with whom he came in contact. His and your unselfish sacrifice in the cause of humanity is a source of admiration and gratitude from all his comrades in the Royal Air Force . . ."

"Up, up the long, delirious, burning blue
   I've topped the wind-swept heights with easy grace,
Where never lark, or even eagle flew—
   And, while with silent, lifting mind I've trod
   The high untrespassed sanctity of space,
Put out my hand and touched the face of God."